SO THERE

Also by Robert Creeley

POETRY

For Love • *Words* • *The Charm* • *Pieces*
A Day Book • *Hello: A Journal* • *Later*
Collected Poems: 1945–1975 • *Mirrors*
Memory Gardens • *Selected Poems*
Windows • *Echoes* • *Life & Death*

FICTION

The Gold Diggers • *The Island*
Presences • *Mabel: A Story*
Collected Prose

DRAMA

Listen

ESSAYS

A Quick Graph: Collected Notes & Essays
Was That a Real Poem & Other Essays
Collected Essays
Autobiography
Tales Out of School

ANTHOLOGIES AND SELECTIONS

The Black Mountain Review 1954–1957
New American Story (with Donald M. Allen)
The New Writing in the U.S.A. (with Donald M. Allen)
Selected Writings of Charles Olson
Whitman: Selected Poems
The Essential Burns
Charles Olson, Selected Poems

ROBERT CREELEY

SO THERE

POEMS 1976-83

A New Directions Book

"Old Poetry," used as the Preface in this volume, will also appear in *99
Poets/1999: An International Poetics Symposium,* ed. Charles Bernstein
(special issue of *boundary 2,* vol. 16:2, 1999). Acknowledgments for
individual volumes appear on p. 248.

Manufactured in the United States of America
New Directions Books are printed on acid-free paper.
First published as New Directions Paperbook 870 in 1998
Published simultaneously in Canada by Penguin Books Canada Limited
Book design by Erik Rieselbach; lettering by Jim Dine

Library of Congress Cataloging-in-Publication Data

Creeley, Robert, 1926–
So There : poems 1976–1983 / Robert Creeley.
    p.   cm. — (New Directions paperback ; 870)
Includes index.
ISBN 0-8112-1397-8 (pbk : acid-free paper)
I. Title.
PS3505.R43S6   1998
811'.54—dc21   98-35576
                                                              CIP

New Directions Books are published for James Laughlin
by New Directions Publishing Corporation,
80 Eighth Avenue, New York, NY 10011

CONTENTS

for Pen

PREFACE: OLD POETRY

> Ay, tear her tattered ensign down!
> Long has it waved on high,
> And many an eye has danced to see
> That banner in the sky;
> Beneath it rung the battle shout,
> And burst the cannon's roar; –
> The meteor of the ocean air
> Shall sweep the clouds no more.
> —Oliver Wendell Holmes

Even to speak becomes an unanticipated drama, because where one has come to, and where it is one now has to go, have no language any longer specific. We all will talk like that, yet no one will understand us.

When I was a young man, I felt often as if I were battling for the integrity of my habits of speech, my words, my friends, my life. W. C. Williams had put it most clearly, and with the expected emphasis of that time: "When a man makes a poem, makes it, mind you, he takes words as he finds them interrelated about him and composes them—without distortion which would mar their exact significances—into an intense expression of his perceptions and ardors that they may constitute a revelation in the speech that he uses." In the furies, then, of the war and the chaos of a disintegrating society, I felt a place, of useful honor and possibility, in those words.

*As though one might dignify, make sufficient, all the bits
and pieces one had been given, all the remnants of a fam-
ily, the confusions of name and person, flotsam, even the
successes quickly subsumed by the next arrival. And after
that, the next—and then the next again. How would one
ever catch up?*

There was no identity, call it, for the poet in my world.
It was only in my mind and imagination that any of it
was real. "Only the imagination is real," Williams said.
It felt particularly American to have no viable tradition,
no consequence of others seemingly sufficient, my elders
contested if not dismissed. Yet, paradoxically, we were
exceptionally chauvinistic, felt finally a contempt for the
poetry of that old world, the European, which nonethe-
less still intimidated us. All the arts, it seemed, fought to
become dominant in whatever scale they might be
weighed in—Abstract Expressionists vs. the School of
Paris, John Cage vs. Benjamin Britten, Louis Zukofsky
vs. W. H. Auden. Already that person as *myself* had be-
come an insistent *we,* a plural of swelling confidence.

*They say you can be sure of three things in America, in any
company, and you can always let them be known without
fear of social reprisal. One, that you know nothing about
opera. Two, that you know nothing about poetry. Three,
that you speak no language other than English. Is that true?*

René Thom somewhere speaks of poetry's being like
humor. It stays local because it uses its means with such
particularity. Just so, a friend tells me of a friend of his,
a fellow student who is Japanese, saying, "What the
Americans think is interesting in Japanese poetry misses
the point entirely. They miss the essence, the kernel, the
substance of its effects." Another friend once told me he
had written a haiku whose second line was a measured
one mile long.

"A Nation of nothing but poetry..." Who owns it? "He is the president of regulation..." How did that go? How is it (ever) far if you think it? Where are we? It was poetry that got us here, and now we have to go too. "I'll hate to leave this earthly paradise..." Is there a country? "Image Nation..."

Despairs since I was a little boy seem always the same. No money, not enough to eat, no clothes, sick, forced out. No job or identity. Years ago, driving back to San Geronimo Miramar from Guatemala City in the early evening, I caught sight of a body lying out into the narrow road, so stopped to see what had happened. It was a man, drunk, trying to kill himself in that bleak way. He had spent all his life's accumulated money in one day's drinking, and had lost his identity card as well—and so he no longer actually existed, in any record. I kept trying, uselessly, persistently, to help.

We will keep ourselves busy enough, working with our various procedures and values. There'll be no irony or blame. Whoever we imagine it's for will either hear us out, else leave with a sense of better things to do. Better we learn a common song?

Seventy-two my next birthday and still feeling good, still pouring it out. Hardly a day goes by that I don't think of something, either to do or to be done. Stay *busy* seems to be it. But most it's like coming back again to childhood, dumbly, even uselessly. When I saw my old school chums at our fiftieth reunion, I realized I hadn't seen them— Fred, Marion, Katie, Ralph and Patsy—since we were fourteen. Now we were over sixty, all the work done but for whatever was left to tidy up. It was a great, unexpected relief not to have to say what we had earned, merited, lost or coveted. It was all done.

So now for the bridge, as in music, carries one over—

> Trust to good verses then;
> They only will aspire,
> When pyramids, as men,
> Are lost i' th' funeral fire.
>
> And when all bodies meet,
> In Lethe to be drowned,
> Then only numbers sweet
> With endless life are crown'd.
>
> —Robert Herrick

With love, for Herrick and Zukofsky.

Buffalo, N.Y.
Feb. 8, 1998

HELLO

A JOURNAL

FEB. 29 - MAY 3
1976

WELLINGTON,
NEW ZEALAND

"That's the way
(that's the way

I like it
(I like it"

•

Clouds coming close.

•

Never forget
clouds dawn's
pink red acid
gash—!

•

Here comes
one now!

•

Step out into
space. Good
morning.

•

Well, sleep,
man.

•

Not *man*,
mum's
the word.

•

What do you
think those hills
are going to do now?

•

They got
all the
lights on—
all the people.

•

You know
if you never
you won't

2/29

It's the scale
that's attractive,
and the water
that's around it.

•

Did the young
couple come
only home
from London?

Where's the world
one wants.

•

Singular,
singular,

one
by one.

•

I wish I
could see the stars.

•

Trees *want*
to be still?
Winds
won't let them?

•

Anyhow,
it's night now.

Same clock ticks
in these different places.

3/1

DUNEDIN

River wandering down
below in the widening green
fields between the hills—
and the sea and the town.

Time settled, or waiting,
or about to be. People,
the old couple, the two babies,
beside me—the so-called

aeroplane. Now
be born,
be born.

•

9

I'll never
see you,
want you,
have you,
know you—

I'll never.

•

"Somebody's got to pay
for the squeaks in the bed."

•

Such quiet,
dog's scratch at door—

pay for it all?

•

Walking
and talking.

Thinking
and drinking.

•

Night.
Light's out.

3/3

"*Summa wancha*

out back"

Australia

•

"Sonny Terry,
"Brownie McGhee"

in Dunedin (in
Dunedin

3/4

10:30 AM: RALPH HOTERE'S

Warm.
See sun shine.
Look across valley at houses.
Chickens squawk.
Bright glint off roofs.
Water's also,
in bay, in distance.
Hills.

3/5

CHRISTCHURCH

You didn't think you
could do it but you did.

You didn't do it
but you did.

•

CATCHING COLD

I want to lay down
and die—
someday—but
not now.

11

•

South, north, east, west,
man—home's best.

•

Nary an exit
in Christchurch.

Only
wee holes.

3/9

OUT WINDOW:
TAYLOR'S MISTAKE

Silver,
lifting
light—

mist's
faintness.

•

FRIEND SAYS OF JOB
for Barry Southam

You get to see all kinds of life
like man chasing wife
in the driveway
with their car.

Mutual property!
They want to sell their house?

·

Elsewise absences,
eyes a grey blue,
tawny Austrian

hair—the voice,
speaking, *there*.

·

Hermione, in the garden,
"weeping at grief?"

Stone-statued single woman—
eyes alive.

·

MILTON ÜBER ALLES

When I consider
how my life is spent
ere half my years
on this vast blast

are o'er...

·

Reasoned recognitions—
feelings fine.

·

Welcome
to the world,
it's still pretty much the same.

That kiwi
on yon roof
is a symbol,
but the ocean

don't change.
It's all *round!*
Don't
let them kid you.

3/11

PALMERSTON NORTH

SOUP

I know what you'd say
if I could ask you—
but I'm tired of it—
no word, nothing again.

Letter from guy says,
"she looks well,
happy, working hard—"
Forget it.

I'm not there.
I'm really here,
sitting,
with my hat on.

It's a great day
in New Zealand
more or less.
I'm not alone in this.

Lady out window hangs clothes,
reds and blues—
basket, small kid,
clothespins in mouth.

Do I want to fuck,
or eat?
No problem.
There's a telephone.

I know what you mean,
now "down under" here,
that each life's
got its own condition

to find,
to get on with.
I suppose it's
letting go, finally,

that spooks me.
And of course my arms
are full as usual.
I'm the only one I know.

May I let this be
West Acton, and
myself six? No,
I don't travel that way

despite memories,
all the dear or awful
passages apparently
I've gone through.

Back to the weather,
and dripping nose
I truly wanted to forget here,
but haven't—

ok, old buddy,
no projections, no regrets.
You've been a dear friend
to me in my time.

If it's New Zealand
where it ends,
that makes a weird sense
too. I'd never have guessed it.

Say that all the ways
are one—*consumatum est*—
like some soup
I'd love to eat with you.

3/16

This wide, shallow bowl,
the sun, earth here
moving easy, slow
in the fall, the air
with its lightness, the
underchill now—flat, far out,
to the mountains and the forest.
Come home to its song?

•

Sitting at table—
good talk
with good people.

•

River's glint, wandering
path of it.

Old trees grown tall,
maintain,
look down on it all.

　　　•

Bye-bye, kid says,
girl, about five—
peering look,
digs my one eye.

　　　•

Sun again, on table,
smoke shaft of cigarette,
ticking watch,
chirr of cicadas—
all world, all mind, all heart.
　　　　　　　　　3/17

WELLINGTON

Here again,
shifting days,

on the street.
The people of my life

faded,
last night's dreams,

echoes now.
The vivid sky, blue,

sitting here in the sun—
could I let it go?

Useless question?
Getting old?

•

I want to be a dog,
when I die—

a dog, a dog.

•

BRUCE & LINLEY'S HOUSE

Fire back of grate
in charming stove
sits in the chimney hole,
cherry red—
but orange too.

•

Mrs. Manhire saw me
on plane to Dunedin,
but was too shy to speak
in her lovely Scots accent.

We meet later,
and she notes the sounds are
not very sweet
in sad old Glasgow.

But my wee toughness,
likewise particularity,
nonetheless come
by blood from that city.

•

LOVE

Will you be dust,
reading this?

Will you be sad
when I'm gone.

3/19

SIT DOWN

Behind things
or in front of them,
always a goddamn
adamant number stands

up and shouts,
I'm here, I'm here!
—Sit down.

•

Mother and son
get up,
sit down.

•

NIGHT

Born and bred
in Wellington
she said—

Light high,
street black,
singing still,

"Born & bred
in Wellington,
she said—"

　　　　•

DOGGIE BAGS

Don't take
the steak
I ain't
Dunedin

　　　　•

The dishes
to the sink
if you've
Dunedin

　　　　•

Nowhere
else to go
no I'm not
Dunedin

　　　　•

Ever if
again home
no roam
(at the inn)

Dunedin

　　　　•

MAYBE

Maybe
this way again

someday—
thinking, last night,

of Tim Hardin, girl singing,
"Let me be your rainy day man..."

What's the time, dear.
What's happening.

    •

Stay

in Dunedin

for

forever

and a day.

    •

Thinking light,
whitish blue,
sun's
shadow on
the porch
floor.

    •

Why, in Wellington,
all the "Dunedin"—

Why here
there.

3/21

HAMILTON

HAMILTON HOTEL

Magnolia tree out window
here in Hamilton—
years and years ago
the house, in France,

called *Pavillion des Magnolias,*
where we lived and Charlotte
was born, and time's gone
so fast—.

    •

Singing undersounds,
birds, cicadas—
overcast grey day.

Lady far off across river,
sitting on bench there,
crossed legs, alone.

    •

If the world's one's
own experience of it,

then why walk around
in it, or think of it.

More would be more
than one could know

alone, more than myself's
small senses, of it.

3/22

AUCKLAND

SO THERE
for Penelope

Da. Da. Da da.
Where is the song.
What's wrong
with life

ever. More?
Or less—
days, nights,
these

days. *What's gone
is gone forever
every time,* old friend's
voice here. I want

to stay, somehow,
if I could—
if I would? Where else
to go.

The sea here's out
the window, old
switcher's house, vertical,
railroad blues, *lonesome*

whistle, etc. Can you
think of Yee's Cafe
in Needles, California
opposite the train

station—can you keep
it ever
together, old buddy, talking
to yourself again?

Meantime some *yuk*
in Hamilton has blown
the whistle on a charming
evening I wanted

to remember otherwise—
the river there, that
afternoon, sitting,
friends, wine & chicken,

watching the world go by.
Happiness, happiness—
so simple. What's
that anger is that

competition—sad!—
when this at least
is free,
to put it mildly.

My aunt Bernice
in Nokomis,
Florida's last act,
a poem for Geo. Washington's

birthday. Do you want
to say "it's bad"?
In America, old sport,
we shoot first, talk later,

or just take you out to dinner.
No worries, or not
at the moment,
sitting here eating bread,

cheese, butter, white wine—
like Bolinas, "Whale Town,"
my home, like they say,
in America. It's *one* world,

it can't be another.
So the beauty,
beside me, rises,
looks now out window—

and breath keeps on breathing,
heart's pulled in
a sudden deep, sad
longing, to want

to stay—be another
person some day,
when I grow up.
The world's somehow

forever that way
and its lovely, roily,
shifting shores, sounding now,
in my ears. My ears?

Well, what's on my head
as two skin appendages,
comes with the package.
I don't want to

argue the point.
Tomorrow
it changes, gone,
abstract, new places—

moving on. Is this
some old-time weird
Odysseus trip
sans paddle—up

the endless creek?
Thinking of you,
baby, thinking
of all the things

I'd like to say and do.
Old-fashioned time
it takes to be
anywhere, at all.

Moving on. Mr. Ocean,
Mr. Sky's
got the biggest blue eyes
in creation—

here comes the sun!
While we can,
let's do it,
let's have fun.

3/26

SIDNEY, AUSTRALIA

NOW

Hard to believe
it's all *me*

whatever
this world

of space & time,
this place,

body,
white,

inutile,
fumbling at the mirror.

3/27

YAH

Sure I fell in love—
"with a very lovely person."
You'd love her too.
"She's lovely."

•

Funny what your head
does, waking up

in room, world,
you never saw before,

each night new.
Beautiful view, like they say,

this time, Sydney—
who's always been a friend of mine.

Boats out there, dig it?
Trees so green you could

eat them, grass too.
People, by god—

"so you finally got here?"
Yeah, passing through.

•

One person
and a dog.

•

Woman staggering
center of street—

wop!
Messy.

All in
the mind.

•

Long
legged
dark
man

I think.

     •

Hey Cheryl!
Talk

to me.
Yiss?

Say it like this.

     •

I love
Australia—

it's so big
and fuzzy

in bed.

     •

THEN

Don't go
to the mountains,

again—not
away, mad. Let's

talk it out, you
never went anywhere.

I did—and here
in the world, looking back

on so-called life
with its impeccable

talk and legs and breasts,
I loved you

but not as some
gross habit, please.

Your voice
so quiet now,

so vacant, for me,
no sound, on the phone,

no clothes, on the floor,
no face, no hands,

—if I didn't want
to be here, I wouldn't

be here, and would
be elsewhere? Then.

3/28

WINDOW

Aching sense
of being

person—body in-
side, out—

the houses, sky,
the colors, sounds.

3/29

PLACES

All but
for me and Paul.

•

Off
of.

3/30

EN ROUTE PERTH

FOR CHERYL

Sitting here in limbo, "there are
sixteen different shades of red."

Sitting here in limbo, there are
people walking through my head.

If I thought I'd think it different,
I'd just be dumber than I said.

•

Hearing sounds in
plane's landing gear lowering:

I don' wanna

3/31

MEN

Here, on the wall
of this hotel in
Singapore, there's a

picture, of a woman,
big-breasted, walking,
blue-coated, with

smaller person—both
followed by a house men
are carrying. It's a day

in the life of the world.
It tells you, somehow,
what you ought to know.

      •

Getting fainter, in the world,
fearing something's fading,
deadened, tentative responses—
go hours without eating,
scared without someone to be
with me. These empty days.

      •

Growth, trees, out window's
reminiscent of other days,

other places, years ago,
a kid in Burma, war,

fascinated, in jungle,
happily not shot at,

hauling the dead and dying
along those impossible roads

to nothing much could help.
Dreaming, of home, the girl

left behind, getting drunk,
getting laid, getting beaten

out of whorehouse one night.
So where am I now.

•

Patience gets
you the next place.

So they say.

•

Some huge clock
somewhere said it was
something like sixteen

or twenty hours later
or earlier there, going
around and around.

•

BLUE RABBIT

Things going quiet
got other things

in mind. That rabbit's
scared of me! I can't

drag it out by the ears
again just to look.

　　　•

I'll remember the dog,
with the varicolored,

painted head, sat
beside me, in Perth,

while I was talking
to the people

in the classroom—
and seemed to listen.

　　　　　　　4/4

MANILA,
THE PHILIPPINES

COUNTRY WESTERN

Faint dusky light
at sunset—park,

Manila—people
flooding the flatness,
speakers, music:

"Yet I did

"the best I could

"with what I had…"

　　　•

HERE AGAIN

No sadness
in the many—
only the one,
separate, looks
to see another
come. So it's
all by myself
again, one
way or another.

·

LATER

Later than any time
can tell me, finding
ways now as I can—

any blame, anything
I shouldn't do, any
thing forgotten, any way

to continue, this little
way, these smaller ways—
pride I had, what I thought

I could do, had done.
Anyone, anything, still
out there—is there some

one possible, something
not in mind still as
my mind, my way. I

persist only in wanting,
only in thinking, only now
in waiting, for that way

to be the way I can
still let go, still want, and
still let go, and want to.

4/5

MANILA

Life goes on living,
sitting in chair here

in café at Domestic Airport—
heat stirring my skin & bones,

and people like dusty
old movie, Peter Lorre, and

I don't see no criminals
looking at nobody, only

myriad people on this final
island of the ultimate world.

•

Each time *sick loss*
feeling starts to hit me,
think of *more* than that,
more than "I" thought of.

•

Early morning still—
"announcing the ah-ri-

val" of world in little,
soft, wet, sticky pieces.

        •

You can tilt the world
by looking at it sideways—

or you can put it up-
side down by standing on

your head—and underneath,
or on end, or this way,

or that, the waves come in,
and grass grows.

        •

BREAKING UP IS
HARD TO DO

"Don't take your love
"away from me—

"Don't leave my heart
"in misery..."

I know that it's
true. I know.

        •

One day here
seems like years now

since plane came in
from Singapore—

heart in a bucket,
head in hand.

　　　　·

Falling to sleep nights
like losing balance—

crash!—wake to bright
sunlight, time to go!

CEBU

CEBU

Magellan was x'ed here
but not much now left,

seemingly, of that event
but for hotel's name—

and fact of boats filling
the channel. And the churches,

of course, as Mexico, as all of
Central and South America.

Driving in from the airport,
hot, trying to get bearings—

witness easy seeming pace of the place,
banana trees, mangos, the high

vine grapes on their trellises.
But particularly the people moseying

along. Also the detention home
for boys, and another casual prison

beside the old airport now
used for light planes. I saw

in a recent paper a picture
of a triangular highrise in Chicago,

downtown, a new prison there,
looking like a modern hotel.

Also in Singapore there are
many, many new buildings—

crash housing for the poor,
that hurtles them skyward off

the only physical thing they
had left. Wild to see clotheslines,

flapping shirts, pants, dresses,
something like thirty stories up!

I'd choose, no doubt dumbly
to keep my feet on the ground—

and I like these houses here,
open-sided, thatched roofed—

that could all be gone in a flash,
or molder more slowly

back into humus. One doesn't
finally want it all forever,

not stopped there, in abstract
time. Whatever, it's got to

be yielded, let go of, it can't
live any longer than it has to.

Being human, at times I
get scared, of dying, growing

old, and think my body's
possibly the exception to all

that I know has to happen.
It isn't, and some of those

bananas are already rotten,
and no doubt there are vacant

falling-down houses, and boats
with holes in their bottoms

no one any longer cares about.
That's all right, and I can

dig it, yield to it, let what
world I do have be the world.

In this room the air-conditioner
echoes the southwest of America—

my mother-in-law's, in Albuquerque,
and I wonder what she's doing

today, and if she's happy there,
as I am here, with these green

walls, and the lights on, and
finally loving everything I know.

4/7

MORNING

Dam's broke,
head's a
waterfall.

DAVAO

DAVAO INSULAR HOTEL

You couldn't get it
off here in a million

obvious years, shrubs cut
to make animals, bluish,

reddish, purple lights
illuminating the pool—

and the only lady within
miles to talk to tells me

she got culture-shocked by
multiple single-seat tv sets

in bus stations, airports, in
the States. So we're single

persons, so the jungle's
shrunk to woods, and

people are Jim and Mary—
have a drink. I can't

believe the solution's this
place either, three hundred

calculated persons to each
and every family unit,

sucking like mad to get fed.
Extended, distended—no

intent ever to be more or
less than the one sits next

to you, holds your hand,
and, on occasion, fucks.

4/8

BALER

APOCALYPSE NOW

Waiting to see if
Manila's a possi-
bility, yellow plane
of Francis F. Coppola
on tarmac fifty
yards away—kids,
coins, flipping, air
wet, rather warm—
no movies today,
friends—just sit
in air, on bench, be-
fore cantina, listen
to words of mouths

talking Tagalog,
and "I swear I
love my husband"—
I could spend quite
a bit of time here,
but by nine in
the morning, I hope
I can get home.

                •

Wrong: white man's
over-reach, teeth
eating tongue, spoken
beforehand, al-
ready.

                                        4/10

SINGAPORE

EVENING

Walking street back here,
the main drag for the money,
and lights just going on,
day faded, people hot, distracted—

one person, walking, feeling older
now, heavier, from chest to hips
a lump won't move with my legs,
and all of it tireder, slower—

flashes in store windows, person
with somewhat silly hat on,
heavy-waisted, *big,* in the company,
and out of step, out of place—

back to the lone hotel room,
sit here now, writing this,
thinking of the next step,
and when and how to take it.

                    •

Split mind, hearing voice—
two worlds, two places.

4/11

TALKING

Faded back last night
into older dreams, some

boyhood lost innocences.
The streets have become inaccessible

and when I think of people,
I am somehow not one of them.

Talking to the doctor-
novelist, he read me a poem

of a man's horror, in Vietnam,
child and wife lost to him—

his own son sat across from me,
about eight, thin, intent—

and myself was like a huge,
fading balloon, that could hear

but not be heard, though we
talked and became clear friends.

I wanted to tell him I was
an honest, caring man. I wanted

the world to be more simple,
for all of us. His wife said,

driving back, that my hotel's bar
was a swinging place in the '50s.

It was a dark, fading night.
She spoke quickly, obliquely,

along for the ride, sitting
in the front seat beside him.

I could have disappeared, gone
away, seen them fading too,

war and peace, death,
life, still no one.

•

Why want
to be so *one*
when it's not
enough?

•

Down and
down, over
and out.

4/13

KUALA LUMPUR,
MALAYSIA

OLD SAYING

There is no
more.

.

Start again
from the beginning then.

4/14

HOTEL LOBBY

Sun out window's
a blessing, air's
warmth and wetness.

The people fade,
melt, in the mind.

.

No scale, no congruence,
enough.

.

This must be some
time-stream, persons
all the same.

.

How call back,
or speak forward?

Keep the physical
literal.

     •

Play on it,
jump up.

     •

I don't
look like
anybody
here!

     •

Funny how
people pick
their noses.

RIDING WITH SAL
for Salleh

Pounding VW motor
past the people, cars—

hot day in downtown
Kuala Lumpur, and the

Chinese-lunch-style
conversation's still in mind,

"do Americans look *down*
on Asians?" Is the world

round, or flat, is it
one, or two, or many—

and what's a Muslim
like you doing here

anyhow. Breeze lifts,
sun brightens at edges,

trees crouch under
towering hotel's walls.

Go to Afghanistan and
be Sufis together, brother,

dance to *that* old in-
veterate wisdom after all.

·

SUFI SAM CHRISTIAN

Lift me into heaven
slowly 'cause my back's

sore and my mind's too
thoughtful, and I'm not

even sure I want to go.

·

LUNCH AND AFTER

I don't want to leave
so quickly, the lovely

faces, surrounding, human
terms so attractive. And

the world, the *world,* we
could think of, *here,* to-

gether, a flash of instant, a
million years of time.

Don't, myself, be an
old man yet, I want to

move out and into this
physical, endless place.

Sun's dazzling shine now
back of the towering clouds,

and sounds of builders'
pounding, faint, distant

buzz of traffic. Mirror's
in front of me, hat's on

head, under it, human
face, my face, reddened,

it seems, lined, grey's
in beard and mustache—

not only *myself* but an-
other man has got to

at last walk out and into
another existence, out there,

that haze that softens those trees,
all those other days to come.

•

WAR & PEACE

Cannot want not to
want, cannot. Thinks

later, acts
now.

     •

HOTEL MERLIN

On the seventeenth
floor of this

modern building, in
room I accepted

gratefully, bed I
lay down on—

vow to think
more responsibly?

Vow to be
kinder to

mother (dead), brothers
(dead), sister—

who loves me?
Will I now see

this world as
possible arrangement.

Will I eat
less, work more

for common ends?
Will I turn from friends,

who are not friends?
Will judgment,

measure
of such order,

rule me?
Or will flash of willful

impulse
still demand

whatever life,
whatever death.

·

SEVENTEENTH FLOOR:
ECHOES OF SINGAPORE

No one's going to
see me naked up here.

My only chance is
to jump.

4/15

UP HERE

Place in mind
or literal, out window,
"too abstract"—

a long way down
to the street—
or home.

•

TIME

Can't live,
mindless,
in present—

can't make past,
or future,
enough place.

4/16

HONG KONG

REMEMBER

Sweltering, close
dreams of a
possible heaven—

before sleeping mind,
before waking
up to dead day.

•

HONG KONG WINDOW

Seemingly awash
in this
place, *here*—

egocentric
abstraction—
no one

else but
me again,
and people,

people as if
behind glass,
close

but untouchable.
What
was the world

I'd thought of,
who
was to be there?

The buildings
lean in
this window,

hotel's abstraction,
cars
like toys pass,

below,
fourteen stories
down

on those streets.
In park
kids wade

in a pool.
Grey day,
in spring,

waits for rain.
"What's
the question?"

Who asks it,
which *me*
of what life.

·

PARK

Like in the Brownie Books—
people below, in distance,
like little moving dots of color,
look at 'em go!

·

Buildings against hillsides
waiting for night
to make a move.

·

Something about the vertical
and the horizontal
out of whack possibly,

viz., the buildings
look like they could walk,
and in the flat park,

below, the people are
walking, and running even,
but I can't put the two together.

•

SIGN

"SIEMENS" not
semen's, and I don't
see men's—and I don't
know what it means.

•

BUILDINGS

Why not make them
higher, and higher, and
higher—until they fall down?

•

Something about raw side
of cut cliff, with building
jammed against it, still hurts.

•

With world now
four billion, you
haven't even started yet.

•

Sentimental
about earth
and water,

and people?
Still got enough
to share?

        •

But if you don't,
you won't
have it long.

        •

The money's singing
in the walls of this building

        •

Sun's out. Big
lazy clouds float
over the buildings.
Thank god.

        •

PARK

Why did that man
fly the kid's kite
precisely into the trees

when a wide space
of bare ground was
a few feet away. Was it

the women, with them,
sitting on the park bench,
didn't want to move.

•

Kid's face, lifting
big yellow speed boat
with proper gas motor

out of pool after
it's conked out, all
the other kids around,

watching him. He's in
some sad defensive place
now. It's still his.

•

Lots of older
women here talking
to younger women.

Now one, by herself,
pregnant, walks by.
Her legs look thin from the back.

•

This park is really used.
It's got bare ground
like in Boston.

•

Can see tennis players,
with roller skaters behind them.
"One world."

•

Trees dancing now.
They dig it.

                .

And you can't
be alone for long.

4/19

HONG KONG— LAST WORDS

I want to get off
the fucking world and
sit down in a chair,
and be there.

4/21

TOKYO, JAPAN

THINGS TO DO IN TOKYO
                for Ted Berrigan

Wake up.
Go to sleep.
Sit *zazen* five days
in five minutes.

Talk
to the beauty next to me
on plane, go-
ing to San Francisco.

Think it's all a dream.
Return
"passport, wallet and ticket"
to man I'd taken them from.

No mistakes.
This time.
Remember mother
ashed in an instant.

No tears.
No way, other than this one.
Wander. Sing
songs from memory. Tell

classical Chinese poet
Bob Dylan's the same.
Sit again in air.
Be American.

Love. Eat
Unspeakable Chicken—
"old in vain."
Lettuce, tomato—

bread. Be humble.
Think again.
Remy Martin is
Pete Martin's brother?

Drink. Think
of meeting Richard Brautigan,
and brandy, years ago.
(All the wonder,

all the splendor,
of Ezra Pound!)
Don't be dismayed,
don't be cheap.

No Hong Kong,
no nothing.
Be on the way
to the way

to the way.
Every day's happy,
sad. "That's the way"
to think. Love

people, all over.
Begin at the beginning,
find the end.
Remember everything,

forget it. Go on,
and on. Find ecstasy,
forget it.
Eat chicken entirely,

recall absent friends.
Love wife
by yourself, love
women, men,

children.
Drink, eat
"and be merry." Sleep
when you can. Dogs

possibly human?—
not cats or birds.
Let all openings be openings.
Simple holes.

Virtue is people,
mind's eye in trees,
sky above,
below's water, earth.

Keep the beat
Confucian—"who
controls." Think man's
possibly beauty's brother,

or husband.
No matter, no mind.
It's here, it's around.
Sing

deliberately.
Love all relations,
be father to daughters,
sons. Respect

wife's previous residence
in Tokyo, stories
she told. All time,
all mind, all

worlds,
can't exist
by definition—
are one.

•

THE WINNER

I'm going to beat
everything I can.

·

AMERICAN LOVE

A big-assed
beauty!

·

MEMORY

A fresh
sea breeze.

·

THE

*[Thinking of L.Z., "That
one could, etc."]*

A's

4/21

KYOTO

INN/KYOTO

Suddenly *here*,
let down, into room,
as if bare—

tea,
and packaged small cake,
food also for thought—

squat
on bottom, floor,
feel heavy—

but sure of place,
in place.
Where time's been,

years, a humor
can't
be absent.

So woman, my age,
who's led me
through corridor,

slides door open,
comes into room again,
laughs

at misunderstanding.
"The bath
tonight?" No,

tomorrow
night. "Eat
Japanese

in the morning?"
Eat—
in the morning.

4/23

FOR BENNY

Kids of Kyoto
visible through split
bamboo screen—

across canal
to street. One lifts
her skirt, blue,

to reveal red underpants
her friend
then examines.

It's a small world,
these subtle
wooden houses,

sliding screens,
mats on floor,
water running

so often within hearing—
all that, and the
keeper of this tiny inn,

a woman, laughs,
thank god, as I crash
from wall to wall.

I'm sitting here,
having seen six
temples this morning,

wondering if I lack
religion. Old man
now passes,

shaved head, grey clothes,
and a woman stops
to look in her purse.

It's just about
four o'clock—
it's grey, shifting clouds,

no rain as yet.
I like it, and I'm happy
to sleep on the floor,

which I do, like a log.
It's truly time
to study the water,

passing, each specific
ripple, flicker
of light—take

everything I know
and put it out there,
where it's got to go.

4/24

LATER

Drunks leaning on your arm,
and the endless drinking
in Japan, and going
to Osaka—

"where the men chew tobacker
and the women wiggy-
waggy-woo…"

•

No way
today.

•

CHEAP THRILL

Write in air
with flourishes.

4/25

SAPPORO

WOMEN

I'll always
look that way
to see
where I'm going.

4/27

SEOUL, KOREA

SEOUL SOUNDS

*for English Literary
Society of Korea*

Weird, flat seeming—
tho' mountains surround—
old Seoul!

And they's got
soul-food
and soul-folk, these

instant Irish.
Syncretic,
someone said, when

I'd asked, was there
Confucian true root?
Much mixed in,

thus, but tough,
hold to it,
push back.

Sentimental,
like Americans—
cry and laugh!

Once in, confusions
grow less,
though day's grey

and I'm stretched,
got to talk
in an hour.

But here
in this room, there's
a peace, and some hope

I can say it,
make words sing
human truth:

If one's still
of many,
then one's not alone—

If one lives
with people,
then one has a home.

•

PLACE
              for Maria

Let's take
any
of the information of

this world and
make a picture,
dig. The

fact of things,
you know, the
edges, pieces

of so-called
reality, will doubtless
surface. So

surfaces—abstract
initial e-
vent—are—

god knows, god
possibly cares, and
now some *other*

"thing" is
the case, viz., "I
love you," now
I'm here.

4/29

MARIA SPEAKS

Still morning
again. "Mendel's
successor"—the

Zen brother
next door
who kept

insects in
a jar—perfected
listening

to things
"spreading their legs,"
"fish tanks filled with bugs."

•

KIDS/SEOUL

Watching incredible kids
cross street, against traffic,
pushing a bike—

little girl leads, hand
on the handlebars—
heart's so content

to be pleased,
to find joy,
like they say,

can be simple.

•

TALK

Talking Ginsbergian
chop-talk's
a pleasure—see

person, find face
right over middle.
Look down for shoes,

legs just above.
Something to look at,
and something to love!

4/30

TAEGU

THERE

Miles back
in the wake,
days faded—

nights sleep seemed
falling down
into some deadness—

killing it,
thinking dullness,
thinking body

was dying.
Then
you changed it.

·

CLOCK

How to live
with some plan
puts the days

into emptiness,
fills time
with time?

·

Not much
left to go on—
it's moving
out.

·

GIFTS

Giving me things,
weights accumulate.

I wish
you wouldn't—

I wish we
could eat

somewhere,
drink.

·

FRIEND

"Father's dead,"
feel flutter,

wings, trying
to beat the dark.

·

GOING HOME

You'll love me
later, after

you've tried
everything else

and got tired.
But body's

catching up,
time's lost

as possibility.
Mind's no longer

a way
tonight.

5/1

SEOUL

Korean slang
for Americans:

"hellos"

•

9:45 AM

Sitting in plane still
in airport, bright

tight sunlight
thru window, guy

sitting in seat alongside,
Japanese, flips pages

of white book. In the aisle
people wander, looking for seats.

•

Nobody here to love
enough to want to.

•

American chichi traveler
just flashed past, her
long brown hair wide open!

•

Catches pillow
flipped to her—

In charge.

•

PROBABLE TRUTH

It's best
to die
when you can.

TOKYO

PLACE

Long gone time—
waves still crash in?
Fall coming on?

•

Shifting head to
make transition, rapid
mind to think it.

•

Halfway to wherever,
places, things
I used to do.

•

OUT HERE

People having a good time
in the duty-free shop,
Tokyo Airport—

can you knock it. Recall
Irving Layton's classic line
re his mother: "her face

was flushed with bargains, etc."
Can't finally think
the world is good guys

and bad guys, tho' these creeps
drive me back into this
corner of the bar—but I'd

choose it anyhow, sit,
hoping for company. A few
minutes ago I was thinking:

"Fuck me, Ruby, right
between the eyes!"
Not any more, it's later,

and is going to get later yet
'fore I get on plane, go home,
go somewhere else at least.

It's raining, outside, in
this interjurisdictional headquarters.
I'm spooked, tired, and approaching

my fiftieth birthday. Appropriately
I feel happy, and sad,
at the same time. I think of

Peter Warshall's amulet I've worn
round my neck for two months now—
turtle, with blue bead cosmos—

that's enough. Nancy Whitefield's
childhood St. Christopher's medal
has stayed safe in the little box

wherein I keep fingernail clippers,
and a collar button, and several
small stones I picked up on a beach.

People still around but
they're fading out now to
get another plane. Hostess,

picking up her several fried chicken
quick lunches, smiles at me,
going past. Guy with spoonbill

blue cap and apparently
American bicentennial mottoes
on front of it, orders a San Miguel

beer. Now he knocks on glass door,
adjacent, I guess his wife's on
the other side. Days, days

and nights, and more of same—
and who wins, loses, never
that simple to figure out.

I'll be a long way away
when you read this—and I won't
remember what I said.

•

DEAR

You're getting fat,
dear.

•

THEN

Put yourself where you'll be
in five hours
and look back

and see if you'd do the same
the way you're doing it
all the time.

•

That's not easy
to think about.

•

It was
once.

•

WHICH IS TO SAY

You could do everything
you could do.

•

Killing time
by not looking
by killing time.

•

JAWS

See one more person
chewing something
I'll eat them both.

•

Kid's giggling
obbligato.

•

No one's going
anywhere.

•

EPIC

Save some room
for my epic.

•

Absence makes
a hole.

•

Any story
begins somewhere

and any other story
begins somewhere else.

•

HERE

Since I can't
kill anyone,
I'd better
sit still.

•

SHE'S BACK!

Styles of drinking, the cool
hand extended, the woman
with the one leg crossed,

sticking out. Now the handsome
one walks off, business
completed. Time to go.

•

If you could look
as good as you could
look, you surely would.

•

EYES

Tall
dark
woman

with
black, wide,
shadowed eyes.

•

Great
shade of orange.

•

I don't do this
for nothing yet.

•

Hours
pass.

•

HERE

Sounds like ball
in bowling alley.

Music's
underneath it.

Clapped
hands.

Hums
of various conversations,

people sitting out
on couches,

wide,
low ceilinged space.

Kimonoed kid
sits on floor with buddy.

•

Three.
Straight up.

•

Each one
trying to stay someone.

EN ROUTE
SAN FRANCISCO

SAY SOMETHING

Say something
to me. "Could you
help me with
this..." Such

possibly the woman's
(Thailand) speech
in aisle adjacent,
plane's body, going

through night. It's
going home, with me—
months passed,
things happened in.

I need some
summary, gloss
of it all, days
later. Last recall

was Bobbie in
the kitchen saying
apropos coat, "If
you don't wear it

now, you never will…"
Or Bobbie, at airport.
re people—
"They all look

like R. Crumb
characters…" It
drifts, it
stays by itself.

•

Friends I've loved
all the time,
Joanne,
Shao—but

not so
simply
now
to name them.

•

I could get drunker
and wiser
and lower
and higher.

•

Peter's
amulet
worked!

•

KYOTO

"Arthur's friend's
a nice man!"

•

MEMORY

Nancy finally
at the kitchen table.

•

BOBBIE

Her voice,
her voice, her
lovely voice…

•

Now's
the time.

•

Watching water
blast up
on window
Provincetown—

clouds, air, trees,
ground,
watching for
the next one.

•

One's so neat
about it.

•

ECHO

Faint, persistent
smell of shit.

•

MOMMY

Kid's been crying
so long.

•

IF YOU'RE GOING
TO HAVE ONE

The Chinese, Koreans,
Filipinos, persons from
Thailand

"are better fathers and mothers."

'

•

ON BOARD

The mommy,
daddy

number.

•

God a
crying
kid.

•

LATER

It feels things
are muddled again
when I wanted
my head straight—

in this empty place,
people sleeping, light
from another person
reading lets me see.

That's talking about it.
This is—this is
where I've been before
and now don't want to go back to.

•

No blaming anyone,
nothing I can't do,
nowhere to be happy
but where I am.

•

Plans—the next
six months
all arranged.

•

You can see her face,
hear her voice,
hope it's happy.

5/3

A NOTE

To move in such fashion through nine countries (Fiji was my first stop, so to speak) in a little over two months is a peculiarly American circumstance, and the record thus provoked is *personal* in a manner not only the effect of my own egocentricity, but, again, a fact of American social reality. The tourist will always be singular, no matter what the occasion otherwise—and there is a sense, I think, in which Americans still presume the world as something to look at and use, rather than to live in. Again and again, I found that other cultural patterns, be they Samoan, Chinese, Malaysian, or Filipino, could not easily think of one as singular, and such familiar concepts as the "nuclear family" or "alienation" had literally to be translated for them. Whereas our habit of social value constantly promotes an isolation—the house in the country, the children in good schools—theirs, of necessity, finds center and strength in the collective, unless it has been perverted by Western exploitation and greed.

Not long ago, reading poems at a communal center in Indianapolis, I was asked by a member of the black community to explain my going to such places as the Philippines and South Korea—where overtly fascist governments are in power—sponsored by our State Department. The same question was put to me by an old friend indeed, Cid Corman, in Kyoto. How could I answer? That I am American? That the government is mine too? I wish I might find so simply a vindication. No, I went because I wanted to—to look, to see, even so briefly, how people in those parts of the world made a reality, to talk of being American, of the past war, of power, of usual life in this country, of my fellow and sister poets, of my neighbors on Fargo Street in Buffalo, New York. I wanted, at last, to be *human,* however simplistic that wish. I took thus my own chances, and remarkably found a company. My deepest thanks to them all.

—R.C.

LATER

Count then your blessings, hold in mind
All that has loved you or been kind...
Gather the bits of road that were
Not gravel to the traveller
But eternal lanes of joy
On which no man who walks can die.
        —from Patrick Kavanagh, "Prelude"

One

MYSELF

What, younger, felt
was possible, now knows
is not—but still
not changed enough—

Walked by the sea,
unchanged in memory—
evening, as clouds
on the far-off rim

of water float,
pictures of time,
smoke, faintness—
still the dream.

I want, if older,
still to know
why, human, men
and women are

so torn, so lost,
why hopes cannot
find better world
than this.

Shelley is dead and gone,
who said,
"Taught them not this—
to know themselves;

their might Could not repress
the mutiny within,
And for the morn
of truth they feigned,

deep night
Caught them ere evening…"

THIS WORLD

If night's the harder,
closer time, days
come. The morning
opens with light

at the window.
Then, as now, sun
climbs in blue sky.
At noon

on the beach
I could watch
these glittering
waves forever,

follow their sound
deep into mind
and echoes—
let light

as air
be relief.
The wind
pulls at face

and hands,
grows cold. What
can one think—
the beach

is myriad stone.
Clouds pass,
grey undersides,
white clusters

of air, all
air. Water
moves at the edges,
blue, green,

white twists
of foam.
What then
will be lost,

recovered.
What
matters as one
in this world?

THE HOUSE

Mas-Soñer
Restaurat—Any—
1920... Old
slope of roof,

gutted windows,
doors, the walls,
with crumbling stucco
shows the mortar

and stones
underneath. Sit
on stone wall adjacent
topped with brick,

ground roundabout's weeds,
red dirt, bare rock.
Then look east
down through valley—

fruit trees in their rows,
the careful fields,
the tops of the other
farmhouses below—

then the city, in haze,
the sea. Look
back in time
if you can—

think of the
myriad people
contained in this instant
in mind. But the well

top's gone, and debris
litters entrance.
Yet no sadness,
no fears

life's gone out.
Could put it all right,
given time,
and need, and money,

make this place sing,
the rooms open
and warm, and spring
come in at the windows

with the breeze—
the white blossom
of apple
still make this song.

LA CONCA

Sand here's like meal—
oats, barley, or wheat—
feels round and specific.

Sun's hot,
just past noon, and sound
of small boat clearing headland

chugs against wash.
Light slants
now on rocks, makes shadows.

Beach is a half-moon's
curve, with bluff,
at far end, of rock—

and firs look like garden
so sharply their tops
make line against sky.

All quiet here,
all small
and comfortable. Boat goes by,

beyond, where sky
and sea meet
far away.

SEA

Ever
to sleep,
returning water.

·

Rock's upright,
thinking.

·

Boy and dog
following
the edge.

·

Come back, first
wave I saw.

·

Older man at
water's edge, brown
pants rolled up,
white legs, and hair.

·

Thin faint
clouds begin
to drift over
sun, im-
perceptibly.

·

Stick stuck
in sand, shoes,
sweater, cigarettes.

·

No home more
to go to.

·

But that line,
sky and sea's,
something else.

•

Adios, water—
for another day.

FLAUBERT'S EARLY PROSE

"Eventually he dies
out of a lack of will to live,
out of mere weariness and sadness..."

And then he is hit by a truck
on his way home from work,

and/or a boulder
pushed down onto him
by lifelong friends of the family
writes FINIS to his suffering—

Or he goes to college,
gets married,
and *then* he dies!

Or finally he doesn't die at all,
just goes on living,
day after day in the same old way...

He is a very interesting man,
this intensively sensitive person,
but he has to die somehow—

so he goes by himself to the beach,
and sits down and thinks,
looking at the water to be found there,

"Why was I born? Why
am I living?"—like
an old song, *cheri*—
and then he dies.

BARCELONA: FEBRUARY 13, 1977

Grave, to the will
of the people,
in the plaza
in front of the cathedral,
at noon dance
the *sardana*—

"two policemen dead,
four arrested"—

ritual, formal,
grave, old and young,
coats left in heap
in the middle
of the circle, wind chill—
dance, to find will.

PLACE

This is an empty landscape,
in spite of its light,
air, water—
the people walking the streets.

I feel faint here,
too far off, too
enclosed in myself,
can't make love a way out.

I need the old-time density,
the dirt, the cold,
the noise through the floor—
my love in company.

SPEECH

Simple things
one wants to say
like, what's the day
like, out there—
who am I
and where.

BEACH

Across bay's loop
of whitecaps,
small seeming black
figures at edge—

one, the smallest,
to the water goes.
Others, behind,
sit down.

AFTER

I'll not write again
things a young man
thinks, not the words
of that feeling.

There is no world
except felt, no
one there but
must be here also.

If that time was
echoing, a vindication
apparent, if flesh
and bone coincided—

let the body be.
See faces float
over the horizon let
the day end.

FOR PEN

Reading, in the chair
in front of the fire
keeps the room both warm
and sparely human—

thinking, to where I've come,
where come from,
from what, from whom—
wanting a meaning.

None to hand but the days
pass here,
in dear company
takes mind of shy comfort.

I want the world
I did always,
small pieces
and clear acknowledgments.

I want to be useful
to someone, I think,
always—if not many,
then one.

But to have it
be echo, feeling
that was years ago—
now my hands are

wrinkled and my hair
goes grey—seems
ugly burden
and mistake of it.

So sing this
weather, passing,
grey and blue
together, rain and sun.

LOVE

There are words voluptuous
as the flesh
in its moisture,
its warmth.

Tangible, they tell
the reassurances,
the comforts,
of being human.

Not to speak them
makes abstract
all desire
and its death at last.

EROTICA

On the path
down here, to the sea,
there are bits

of pages
from a magazine, scattered,
the *big tits*

of my adolescence
caught on bushes,
stepped on, faces

of the women, naked,
still smiling out at me
from the grass.

In the factory,
beside which
this path goes,

there is
no one. The windows
are broken out.

A dump
sits in front of it.
Two piles of dirt

beyond that.
Do these
look like tits

too, some primordial
woman sunk
underground

breaking out,
up,
to get me—

shall I throw
myself down
upon it,

this ground
rolls and twists,
these pictures

I want still
to see. Coming back
a day later,

kids were stopped
at that spot
to look

as I would
and had—there the fact
of the mystery

at last—
"what they look like
underneath"—

paper shreds,
blurred pages,
dirty pictures.

NATURE
        for R.B.K.

Out door here—
tall as wall
of usual room,
slight arch at top—

sunlight
in courtyard
beyond
settles on stump

of tree's trunk—
limbs all cut
to force growth,
come summer—

in blue and white
checkerboard tiled
square planter
at bottom

sits in cement,
thoughtful,
men's minded
complement.

THINKING OF WALTER
BENJAMIN

What to say
these days
of crashing disjunct,
whine, of separation—

Not abstract—
"God's will," not
lost in clouds this
experienced wisdom.

Hand and mind
and heart one
ground to walk on,
field to plow.

I know
a story
I can tell
and will.

WAITING FOR A BUS
"EN FRENTE DE LA IGLESIA"

Here's the church,
here's the tower, the wall,
chopped off. *Open*

the door—no
people. This is
age, long time gone,

like town gate sits
at intersection
across—just façade

leading nowhere.
Zipzap, the cars
roar past. Three

faded flags flap
on top of Hotel
Florida. Old dog,

old friend, walks toward us,
legs rachitic, stiff,
reddish hair all fuzzed.

Long grey bus
still parked to go
to Gerona

which, 8th century,
Charlemagne came personally
to take back from Moors.

You can *read
all about it!*
but wind's cold

in this early spring sun,
and this bench's
lost its bars

on the back
but for one—
and bus

now starts up,
and we're on,
and we're gone.

NEWS OF THE WORLD

Topical questions,
as the world swirls,
and never

enough in hand,
head, to know
if Amin

will truly become
"Jimmy Carter's best friend"
as he professes. The facts

are literal daily horror:
⅕ of world's population has no access
to processed drinking water;

"women in rural Burma
walk 15 miles a day to get some
and bring it home,
a six hour trip." Or

Romania's earthquake dead—
"What day is today
and how are my parents?"

were the first words of Sorin Crainic
when he emerged from the rubble
after eleven days. "I kept

hoping all the time.
My hope has come true.
I shall be able to walk again

and breathe fresh air, much
fresh air.
I shall go back to work."

Meanwhile, same page, "Goldwater
Denounces Report Linking Him
To Gang Figures"—"A 36-member

team of journalists from 23 newspapers
and broadcast outlets... continuing
work begun by reporter Don Bolles...

who was murdered last June. One man
has pleaded guilty to second-degree
murder in the killing; two

are awaiting trial." G. believes
"that the reporters had gone to Arizona
hoping to solve the Bolles murder"

but when "they could not" did
"a job" on said state. Too late,
too little. But not for you, Mr. G.,

as hate grows, lies, the same
investment of the nice and tidy
ways to get "rich,"

in this "world,"
wer eld, the length
of a human life.

MORNING

Shadows, on the far wall,
of courtyard, from the sun
back of house, faint

traceries, of the leaves,
the arch of the balcony—
greens, faded white,

high space of flat
blind-sided building
sits opposite this

window, in high door,
across the floor here
from this table

where I'm sitting, writing,
feet on cold floor's
tiles, watching this light.

THE TABLE

Two weeks from now
we'll be gone. Think,
problems will be
over, the time here

done. What's the time
left to be.
Sky's grey again,
electric stove whirs

by the wall with its
snowflake, flowerlike
yellow, blue and green
tile design. On the table

the iris have opened,
two wither and close.
Small jug holds them,
green stalks, husks and buds.

Paper, yesterday's, book
to read face down, ashtray,
cigarettes, letter from
your mother, roll now

of thunder outside. You
put down the papers,
go back to reading
your book, head bent.

Sarah's cap on your hair
holds it close—red at top,
in a circle, first ring French
blue, then one lighter,

then the darker repeated.
Think of the sounds,
outside, now quiet,
the kids gone back to school.

It's a day we may
live forever, this
simple one. Nothing
more, nothing less.

CHILDISH

Great stories matter—
but the one who tells them
hands them on
in turn to another

who also will.
What's in the world
is water, earth,
and fire, some people,

animals, trees, birds,
etc. I can see
as far as you,
and what I see I tell

as you told me
or have or will.
You'll see too
as well.

ECHOES

Eight panes
in this window
for God's light,
for the outside,

comes through door
this morning.
Sun makes laced
shadows on wall

through imperfect glass.
Mind follows,
finds the lines,
the wavering places.

Rest wants
to lie down
in the sun,
make resolution.

Body sits single,
waiting—
but for what
it knows not.

Old words
echoing what
the physical
can't—

"Leave love,
leave day,
come
with me."

REFLECTIONS

What pomposity
could say only—
*Look
at what's happened to me.*

All those others
surrounding
know
the same bounds.

Happiness
finds itself
in one or many
the same—

and dead,
no more than one
or less
makes a difference.

I was thinking
this morning
again—
So be it.

NEW MOON

Are there still some
"quiet craters of the moon"—
seeing that edge of it
you were pointing to,

stopped, in the street,
looking past the wires
on those poles, all
the stores, open, people,

cars, going past, to see
in that space, faint sliver
of its visible edge. What
advice then remembered,

what had she said?
Turn your money over
and bow three times
to make it increase.

LATER

If I could get
my hands on
a little bit
of it—neither fish,

flesh, nor fowl. Not
you, Harry. No one's
mother—or father,
or children. Not

me again. Not
earth, sky, water—
no mind, no time.
No islands in the sun.

Money I don't want.
No place more
than another—
I'm not here

by myself. But,
if you want to give
me something for Xmas,
I'll be around.

NIGHT TIME

When the light leaves
and sky's black,
no nothing
to look at,

day's done.
That's it.

PEACE

You're looking at a chopper,
brother—no words to say.
Just step on
the gas, man, up and away.

That's dead, I know,
I don't even talk like that
any more. My teeth
are hurting.

But if you'll wait
out back, and
hit yourself over the head
with a hard object,

you'll dig, like, you
like me were young once,
jesus, here come
the creeps. I wrote

a book once, and was
in love with
substantial objects.
No more, I can

get out of here
or come here
or go there
or here, in five minutes.

Later. This
is just to say I was
something or other, and you dig it,
that's it, brother.

BLUES

for Tom Pickard

Old-time blues
and things to say—
not going home
till they come to get me.

See the sky
black as night,
drink what's
there to drink.

God's dead,
men take over,
world's round,
all over.

Think of it,
all those years,
no one's the wiser
even older.

Flesh, flesh,
screams in body,
you know,
got to sleep.

Got to eat, baby,
got to.
No way
you won't.

When I lay down
big bed
going to pillow
my sleeping head.

When I fall,
I fall,
straight down deep
I'm going.

No one
touch me
with
their doubting mind.

You don't
love me
like you
say you do, you

don't do me
like you
said
you would.

What I say
to people
don't mean
I don't love,

what I
do don't
do, don't don't
do enough.

Think I drink
this little glass,
sit on my ass,
think about

life, all
those things,
substance.
I could touch you.

Times in jail
I was scared
not of being hurt
but that people lock you up,

what's got to be
cruel is you know,
and I don't, you say
you got the truth.

I wouldn't listen
if I was drunk, couldn't hear
if I was stoned,
you tell me right or don't.

Come on home, brother,
you make a fool,
get in trouble, end up
in jail.

I'm in the jailhouse now.
When they lock the door,
how long is what
you think of.

Believe in what's there,
nowhere else it will be.
They kill you,
they kill me.

Both dead,
we'll rise again.
They believe in Christ,
they'll believe in men.

SPRING IN SAN FELIU

Think of the good times—
again. Can't let it all
fail, fall apart, at
that always vague edge is

the public so-called condition,
which nobody knows enough
ever, even those
are supposed to be it.

I could identify that man,
say, bummed us out, or
the woman took the whole
street to walk in. They are

familiar faces, anywhere. They
don't need a place. But,
quieter, the kid took the running
leap past us, to show off,

the one then asked to look in
to the courtyard, saw the house,
said, *que casa grande!*, sans malice
or envy, the ones let us off

the hook of the randomly purposive
traveler, the dogs that
came with us, over hill,
over dale, the country men and women

could look up from those
rows of stuff they had planted,
showed now green, in the sun,
—how modest those farms and those lives.

Well, walk on... We'll be gone
soon enough. I'll have got
all I wanted—your time and your love
and yourself—like, *poco a poco*.

That sea never cared about us.
Nor those rocks nor those hills,
nor the far-off mountains still
white with snow. The sun

came with springtime—*la
primavera,* they'll say, when
we've gone. But we came.
We've been here.

4/1/77

SPARROWS

Small birds fly up
shaft of stairwell,

sit, chirping,
where sun strikes in at top.

Last time we'll see them,
hear their feisty greeting

to the day's first light,
the coming of each night.

END

End of page,
end of this

company—wee
notebook kept

my mind in hand,
let the world stay

open to me
day after day,

words to say,
things to be.

Two

FOR JOHN CHAMBERLAIN

They paid my way here
and I'll get myself home.
Old saying:
Let the good times roll.

    …

This is Austin
spelled with an H? This is
Houston, Texas—
Houston Street is back there—

ways in and out
of New York. The billboards
are better than the natural view,
you dig. I came here

just to see you, personal
as God and just as real.
I may never go home
again. Meantime

the lead room with the x
number of people
under the street
is probably empty tonight.

In New York, in
some other place.
Many forms.
Many farms, ranches

in Texas—many places,
many miles, big
endless spaces they say.
This is Marlboro Country

with box those dimensions,
module. Old movie of you
using baler with the crunchers
coming down so delicately.

The kids in the loft, long space.
The Oldenbergs going to work,
eight o'clock. Viva
talking and talking. Now I'm

stoned again, I was
stoned again, all that
past, years
also insistent dimension.

If I could take the world,
and put it on its side, man,
and squeeze just in the right
places. Wow. I don't think

much of interest would happen.
Like the lion coming into the room
with two heads, we'd all end up
killing it to see it.

So this is Art and here we are.
Who would have thought it?
I'll go sooner than you.
I can always tell

no matter how long I sit
after they've all gone, but the bottle
isn't empty.
No one's going to throw me out.

Let's sit in a bar and cry again.
Fuck it! Let's go out on your boat
and I'll fall asleep just like
they all do you tell me.

Terrific. Water's
an obvious material.
You could even make
a suit out of it. You could

do anything you wanted to,
possibly, if you wanted to.
Like coming through customs
with the grey leather hat.

It's all so serious and wonderful.
It's all so big and small.
Upended, it begins again, all the way
from the end to the very beginning,

again. I want it two ways,
she said, in a book
someone wrote. I want it all.
I want to take it all home.

But there's too much already
of everything, and something
I have to let go
and that's me, here and now.

But before leaving, may I say
that you are a great artist
whatever that turns out to be,
and art is art because of you.

I LOVE YOU

I see you, Aunt Bernice—
and your smile anticipating reality.
I don't care any longer that you're older.
There are times all the time the same.

I'm a young old man here on earth,
sticks, dust, rain, trees, people.
Your cat killing rats in Florida was incredible—
Pete—weird, sweet presence. Strong.

You were good to me. You had *wit*—
value beyond all other human possibility.
You could smile at the kids, the old cars.
Your house in N.H. was lovely.

FOUR YEARS LATER

When my mother
died, her things were
distributed

so quickly. Nothing
harsh about it,
just gone,

it seemed, but
for small
mementos, pictures

of family, dresses,
a sweater,
clock.

Looking back
now, wish
I'd talked

more to her.
I tried
in the hospital

but our habit
was too deep—
we didn't

speak easily.
Sitting
now, here,

early morning,
by myself,
can hear her—

as, "Bob,
do what you have to—
I trust you—"

words like
"presumption," possibly
"discretion"—some

insistent demand to
cover living
with clothes—not

"dressed up" but
common, faithful—
what no other can know.

HEAVEN

If life were easy
and it all worked out,
what would this sadness
be about.

If it was happy
day after day,
what would happen
anyway.

NEIGHBORS

Small horses on windowsill
adjacent, 'cross street,
kid's apparent

window, three point
one way, one
another, to face

babydoll, sits there,
with curtains drawn.
Everyone's gone.

JULY: FARGO STREET

Bangs in street.
Fourth's here again,
200th yet,

useless as ever,
'cept for energies
of kids, and the

respite from work
for all these
surrounding neighbors.

THINKING OF YEATS

Break down
"innocence"—
tell truth,

be *small*
in world's
wilderness.

P—

Swim
on her
as in
an ocean.

.

Think out
of it—

be here.

.

Hair's
all around,

floats
in flesh.

.

Eyes'
measure,

mouth's small
discretion.

Smiles.

     •

Long warmth,
speaks

too.

     •

Couldn't
do it
better.

     •

Can walk
along.

BLUE SKIES MOTEL

Look at
that motherfucking smokestack

pointing
straight up.

See those clouds,
old-time fleecy pillows,

like they say, whites and greys,
float by.

There's cars
on the street,

there's a swimming pool
out front—

and the trees
go yellow

now
it's the fall.

RIDDLE

What'd you throw it on the floor for?
Who the hell you think you are

come in here
push me around.

FOR PEN

Thinking out
of the heart—

it's up,
it's down…

It's that time
of day light

echoes the sun
setting west

over mountains.
I want to come home.

CIANO'S

Walking
off street

into Ciano's—
last sun

yellow
through door.

The bar
an oval, people—

behind is
pool table.

Sitting
and thinking.

Dreaming
again

of blue eyes,
actually green—

whose head's
red, mouth's

round, soft
sounds—

whose waist is
an arrow

points down
to earth.

TRAIN GOING BY
for Rosalie Sorrels

When I was a kid
I wanted to get educated
and to college go
to learn how to know.

Now old I've found
train going by
will take me along
but I still don't know why.

Not just for money
not for love
not for anything thought
for nothing I've done—

it's got to be luck
keeps the world going round
myself moving on
on that train going by.

FOR PEN

Last day of year,
sky's a light

open grey, blue
spaces appear

in lateral tiers.
Snow's fallen,

will again. Morning
sounds hum, inside,

outside, roosters squawk,
dog barks, birds squeak.

—"Be happy with me."

LONER

Sounds, crank
of kid's cart's axle

on street, one
floor down.

Heat's thick,
sun's bright

in window still
early morning,

May, fifty-first
birthday. What

time will the
car be done, time—

ready? Sits opposite,
love, in red wrapper,

sheen of silk,
sideways, hair, hands,

breasts, young
flight of fancy,

long fingers, here
in a way

wants the dream back,
keeps walking.

B.B.

What's gone,
bugger all—

nothing lost
in mind till

it's all
forgotten.

MORNING

Light's bright glimmer,
through green bottle

on shelf
above. Light's white

fair air,
shimmer,

blue summer's
come.

THANKS

Here's to Eddie—
not unsteady
when drunk,
just thoughtful.

Here's to his mind
can remember
in the blur
his own forgotten line.

Or, too, lest
forgot, him in the traffic
at Cambridge, outside,
lurching, confident.

He told me later,
"I'm Catholic,
I'm queer,
I'm a poet."

God bless him,
God love him,
I say,
praise him

who saves you time,
saves you money,
takes on the burden
of your own confessions.

And my thanks again
for the cigarettes
he gave me
someone else had left.

I won't escape
his conversation
but will listen
as I've learned to,

and drink
and think again
with this dear man
of the true, the good, the dead.

THERESA'S FRIENDS

From the outset
charmed by the soft, quick speech
of those men and women,
Theresa's friends—and the church

she went to, the "other,"
not the white plain Baptist
I tried to learn God in.
Or, later, in Boston the legend

of "being Irish," the lore, the magic,
the violence, the comfortable
or uncomfortable drunkenness.
But most, that endlessly present talking,

as Mr. Connealy's, the ironmonger,
sat so patient in Cronin's Bar,
and told me sad, emotional stories
with the quiet air of an elder

does talk to a younger man.
Then, when at last I was twenty-one,
my mother finally told me
indeed the name *Creeley* was Irish—

and the heavens opened, birds sang,
and the trees and the ladies spoke
with wondrous voices. The power of the glory
of poetry—was at last mine.

LATER

LATER (1)

Shan't be winding
back in blue
gone time ridiculous,
nor lonely

anymore. Gone,
gone—wee thin
delights, hands
held me, mouths

winked with white
clean teeth. Those
clothes have fluttered
their last regard

to this passing
person walks by
that flat back-
yard once and for all.

LATER (2)

You won't want to be early
for passage of grey mist
now rising from the faint

river alongside the childhood
fields. School bell rings,
to bring you all in again.

That's mother sitting there,
a father dead in heaven,
a dog barks, steam of

drying mittens on the stove,
blue hands, two doughnuts
on a plate.

LATER (3)

The small
spaces of existence,
sudden

smell of burning
leaves makes
place in time

these days
(these days)
passing,

common
to one
and all.

LATER (4)

Opening
the boxes packed
in the shed,

at the edge
of the porch
was to be

place to sit
in the sun,
glassed over,

in the winter
for looking out
to the west,

see the shadows
in the early
morning lengthen,

sharp cold
dryness of air,
sounds of cars,

dogs, neighbors,
persons
of house, toilet

flush, pan
rattle, door
open, never done.

LATER (5)

Eloquent,
my heart,

thump bump—
My Funny Valentine

LATER (6)

If you saw
dog pass, in car—

looking out, possibly
indifferently, at you—

would you—*could* you—
shout, "Hey, Spot!

It's me!" After all
these years,

no dog's coming home
again. Its skin's

moldered
through rain, dirt,

to dust, hair alone
survives, matted tangle.

Your own, changed,
your hair, greyed,

your voice not the one
used to call him home,

"Hey Spot!" *The world's
greatest dog*'s got

lost in the world,
got lost long ago.

LATER (7)

Oh sadness,
boring

preoccupation—
rain's wet,

clouds
pass.

LATER (8)

Nothing "late" about the
"no place to go" old folks—

or "hell," or
"Florida this winter."

No "past" to be
inspired by "futures,"

scales of the imperium,
wonders of what's next.

When I was a kid, I
thought like a kid—

I *was* a kid,
you dig it. But

a hundred and fifty years later,
that's a whole long time to

wait for the train.
No doubt West Acton

was improved by the discontinuance
of service, the depot taken down,

the hangers-around there moved
at least back a street to Mac's Garage.

And you'll have to drive your own car
to get to Boston—or take the bus.

These days, call it "last Tuesday,"
1887, my mother was born,

and now, sad to say,
she's dead. And especially "you"

can't argue
with the facts.

LATER (9)

Sitting up here in
newly constituted

attic room 'mid
pipes, scarred walls,

the battered window
adjacent looks out

to street below. It's fall,
sign woven in iron

rails of neighbor's porch:
"Elect Pat Sole."

O sole mio, mother,
thinking of old attic,

West Acton farmhouse,
same treasures here, the boxes,

old carpets, the smell.
On wall facing, in chalk:

KISS ME. I love you.
Small world of these pinnacles,

places ride up in these
houses like clouds,

145

and I've come as far,
as high, as I'll go.

Sweet weather,
turn now of year...

The old horse chestnut,
with trunk a stalk like a flower's,

gathers strength to face winter.
The spiked pods of its seeds

start to split, soon will drop.
The patience, of small lawns, small hedges,

papers blown by the wind,
the light fading, gives way

to the season. School's
started again. Footsteps fall

on sidewalk down three
stories. It's man-made

endurance I'm after,
it's love for the wear

and the tear here,
goes under, gets broken, but stays.

Where finally else
in the world come to rest—

by a brook, by a
view with a farm

like a dream—in
a forest? In a house

has walls all around it?
There's more always here

than just me, in this room,
this attic, apartment,

this house, this world,
can't escape.

LATER (10)

In testament
to a willingness

to *live,* I,
Robert Creeley,

being of sound body
and mind, admit

to other preoccupations—
with the future, with

the past. But now—
but now the wonder of life is

that *it is* at all,
this sticky sentimental

warm enclosure,
feels place in the physical

with others,
lets mind wander

to wondering thought,
then lets go of itself,

finds a home
on earth.

—400 Fargo
Buffalo, N.Y.
Sept. 3rd–13th, 1977—

FOR RENE RICARD

Remote control factors
of existence, like
"I wanted it this way!"

And hence to Lenox
one summer's day
with old friend, Warren Tallman,

past charming hills
and valleys give class
to that part of western Mass.

I can get funny—
and I can get lost,
go wandering on,

with friends like signboards
flashing past
in those dark nights of the soul.

All one world, Rene,
no matter one's half
of all it is or was.

So walking with you and Pepi,
talking, gossiping,
thank god—the useful news—

what's presently the word
of X, Y, and Z
in NYC, the breezes

on the hill, by the orchard
where Neil sits under tree,
blow the words away,

while he watches me talk,
mouth poems for them,
though he can't hear a word.

This is art,
the public act
that all those dirt roads lead to,

all those fucking bogs
and blown-out tires
and broken fan belts—

willed decision—
call it,
though one's too dumb to know.

For me—and possibly
for only me—a bird
sits in a lousy tree,

and sings and sings
all goddamn day,
and what I do

is write it down,
in words
they call them:

him, and *it,* and *her,*
some story this
will sometimes tell

or not. The bird
can't care, the
tree can hardly hold it up—

and me is least of all
its worry. What then
is this life all about.

Simple. It's garbage
dumped in street,
a friend's quick care,

someone who hates you
and won't go way,
a breeze

blowing past Neil's
malfunctioning dear ears,
a blown-out dusty room,

an empty echoing kitchen,
a physical heart
which goes or stops.

For you—
because you carry wit with you,
and you are there somehow

at the hard real times,
and you know them too—
a necessary love.

THE PLACE

... Swoop of hawk—
or mind's adjustment

to sight—*memory?*
Air unrelieved, *unlived?*

Begun again, begin
again the play

of cloud, the lift
of sudden cliff,

the place in place—
the way it was again.

Go back a day,
take everything, take time

and play it back
again, the staggering

path, ridiculous, uncertain
bird, blurred, fuzzy

fog—or rocks which
seem to hang in

imperceptible substance
there, or here,

in thought? This thinking
is a place itself

unthought, which comes
to be the world.

LEARNING

"Suggestion/recognition..."
The horse
at the edge of the pool,

or the horse's ass,
the fool,
either end, sits

waiting for world
to resolve it—
Or in swirl

of these apparent facts,
contexts, states,
of possible being,

among all others,
of numbered time,
one or two

gleam clearly
there, now *here*—
in mind.

CORN CLOSE
for Basil Bunting

Words again, rehearsal—
"Are we going
to get up *into*

heaven—after all?
What's
the sound of *that*,

who, where—
and how.
One wonder,

one wonders, sees
the world—
specifically, this one.

Sheep, many
with lambs,
of a spring morning,

on sharp slope of hill's side,
run up it
in chill rain.

Below's brook,
as I'd say,
a *burn?* a *beck?*

Goddamnit, *learn* it.
Fell fills eye,
as we lie abed.

Basil's up and out
walking
with the weather's

vagaries. His home is
this world's
wetness

or any's, feet
planted on ground,
and but

for trash can takes
weekly hauling
up and down,

no seeming fact
of age presently
bothers him.

Vague palaver.
Can I get the fire
to burn with wet wood?

Am I useful
today? Will I fuck up
the fireplace?

Drop
log
on my foot.

At breakfast we sit,
provided, tea's steam,
hot scones, butter,

marmalade—Basil's
incurious, reassuring
smile—*and* stories

of Queen E's
garden party, the thousands
jammed into garden—

style
of a damned poor
sort... Consider

(at night) Corelli
gives lifetime
to getting it right:

the *Twelve Concerti Grossi*,
not Ives
(whom I love),

not makeshift,
tonal blather—
but sound meets sound

with clear edge,
finds place,
precise, in the mind.

Have you seen a hawk—
look out! It
will get you,

blurred,
patient person,
drinking, eating,

sans body, sans
history, in-
telligence, etc.

Oh, I think
the words come from
the world and go

"I know
not
where…"

Their breasts banging—
flap—on their breastbones
makes the dear *sound*—

like tire tread
pulled from the shoe—
flap flap, bangs the body,

chortles, gurgles,
wheezes, breathes,
"Camptown race is (?)

five miles long!"
Back on the track,
you asshole.

No excuses,
no
"other things to do"—

And Wyatt's
flight through the night
is an honest

apprehension:
They *flee*
from *me*

that sometime did me seek...
When we'd first come,
our thought

was to help him,
old friend, and brought
such scanty makeshift

provision, in retrospect
I blush—as who
would give to Northumbrian

Teacher's
as against Glenfiddich—
which he had.

Was I scared
old friend
would be broken

by world
all his life
had lived in,

or that art,
his luck,
had gone sour?

My fear
is my own.
He got

the car started
after I tried
and tried, felt

battery fading,
mist-sodden spark plugs—
despair!

He had a wee can
in his hand,
and he sprayed

minute part
of its contents—
phfft!—on car's motor,

and car starts,
by god. What wonder
more than

to be where you are,
and to know it?
All's here.

THE CHILDREN
after Patrick Kavanagh

Down on the sidewalk recurrent
children's forms, reds, greens,
walking along with the watching
elders not their own.

It's winter, grows colder and colder.
How to play today without sun?
Will summer, gone, come again?
Will I only grow older and older?

Not wise enough yet to know
you're only here at all
as the wind blows, now
as the fire burns low.

Three

DESULTORY DAYS
for Peter Warshall

Desultory days,
time's wandering
impermanences—

like, *what's for lunch,*
Mabel? Hunks
of unwilling

meat got chopped
from recalcitrant
beasts? "No tears

for this vision"—
nor huge strawberries
zapped from forlorn Texas,

too soon, too soon...
We will meet again
one day, we will

gather at the river
(Paterson perchance)
so turgidly oozes by,

etc. Nothing new in the world
but us, the human
parasite eats up

that self-defined reality
we talked about in
ages past. Now prophecy declares,

got to get on with it,
back to the farm, else die
in streets inhuman

'spite we made them every one.
Ah friends, before I die,
I want to sit awhile

upon this old world's knee,
yon charming hill, you see,
and dig the ambient breezes,

make of life
such gentle passing pleasure!
Were it then wrong

to avoid, as might be said,
the heaped-up canyons of the dead—
L.A.'s drear smut, and N.Y.C.'s

crunched millions? I don't know.
It seems to me
what can salvation be

for less than 1%
of so-called population
is somehow latent fascism

of the soul. What leaves behind
those other people,
like they say,

reneges on Walter Whitman's
19th century Mr. Goodheart's
Lazy Days and Ways In Which

we might still *save the world*.
I loved it but
I never could believe it—

rather, the existential
terror of New England
countrywoman, Ms.

Dickinson: "The Brain, within its Groove
Runs evenly—and true—
But let a Splinter swerve—

"'Twere easier for You—//
To put a Current back—
When Floods have slit the Hills—

"And scooped a Turnpike for Themselves—
And Trodden out the Mills—"
moves me. My mind

to me a nightmare is—
that thought of days,
years, went its apparent way

without itself, with
no other company than thought.
So—*born to die*—why

take everything with us?
Why the meagerness
of life deliberately,

why the patience
when of no use,
and the anger, when it is?

I am no longer
one man—
but an old one

who is human again
after a long time,
feels the meat contract,

or stretch, upon bones,
hates to be alone
but can't stand interruption.

Funny
how it all works out,
and Asia is

after all *how much money
it costs*—
either to buy or to sell it.

Didn't they have a
world too? But then
they don't look like us,

do they? But they'll get us,
someone will—they'll find us,
they won't leave us here

just to die
by ourselves
all alone?

ARROYO

Out the window,
across the ground there,
persons walk
in the hard sun—

Like years ago we'd watch
the children go to school
in the vacant building now
across the arroyo.

Same persons,
Mr. Gutierrez and,
presumably, his son,
Victor, back from the army—

Would wave to me
if I did to them,
call *que tal, hello,*
across the arroyo.

How sentimental,
heartfelt, this life becomes
when you try to think of it,
say it in simple words—

How far in time and space
the distance,
the simple division of a ditch,
between people.

FOR JOHN DUFF

> "I placed a jar in Tennessee..."
> —Wallace Stevens,
>   "Anecdote of the Jar"

Blast of harsh
flat sunlight

on recalcitrant ground
after rain. Ok.

Life in N.M. is
not a tourist's paradise,

not the solar
energy capital

of the world, not
your place in the sun. If

I had my way,
I'd be no doubt

long gone. But
here I am and we talk

of plastic America,
of other friends

other places. What
will we do

today. When
will heart's peace

descend in rippling, convenient
waves. Why

is the sky still
so high.

What's
underfoot.

I don't
feel comfortable with Indians—

and the Mexican
neighbors with

seventeen kids—
what time exists

now still to
include them.

Ok. A day
goes by. Night

follows. On the slight
lip of earth

down from the gate
at the edge of

the arroyo
sits

a *menhir*—
remember

that oar
you could screw into

ground, say,
here I'll build a city?

No way.
This column

is common
old stretcher

cement blocks.
Put one on one

in pairs, first this way,
then that, you get

a house,
explicit, of the mind,

both thought
and the senses provoke it—

you see it—
you feel and think

this world.
It's a quiet

grey column,
handsome—"the one

missing color"—
and it's here now

forever,
no matter

it falls in a day.
Ok, John.

When you're gone,
I'll remember

also forever
the tough dear

sentiment, the clarity,
of your talking, the care.

And this *it*
you gave us:

here
is all the wonder,

there
is all there is.

TALK

One thing, strikes in,
recall, anyone talking
got to be to human

or something, like a rock,
a "song," a thing to
talk to, to talk to.

POOR

Nothing's
today and
tomorrow only.

            •

Slow-
er.

            •

Place-
ss.

POOR
Pur-
pose por-
puss.

•

Sore hand.

•

Got
to get going.

•

And I was
not asleep

and I was
not alone.

TOUCHSTONE
                for L.Z.

"Something
by which
all else
can be measured."

Something
by which
to measure
all else.

MORNING (8:10 AM)

In sun's
slow rising
this morning

antenna tower
catches
the first light,

shines
for an instant
silver

white,
separate
from the houses,

the trees,
old woman walking
on street out front.

EYE O' THE STORM

Weather's a funny
factor, like once

day breaks, storm's
lifted, or come,

faces, eyes,
like clouds drift

over this world,
are all there is

of whatever there is.

ON A THEME BY LAWRENCE,
HEARING PURCELL

Knowing what
knowing is,

think less
of your life as labor.

Pain's increase,
thought's random torture,

grow with intent.
Simply live.

THIS DAY

This day after
Thanksgiving the edge
of winter
comes closer.

This grey, dulled
morning the sky
closes down on
the horizon to make

one wonder
if a life lives more
than just looking,
knowing nothing more.

Yet such a gentle
light, faded,
domestic,
impermanent—

one will not
go farther than home
to see this world
so quietly, greyly, shrunken.

THE LAST MILE
for Jack Clarke

What's to be said
of friend dead—
eight years later?

Should he have waited
for whatever
here comes together

to make a use
for these friends and fools
must need excuse

for testament, for
interpretation,
for their own investment?

You know the world
is one *big blow*—
that's all.

I'm here as well, now
unable to say
what it is or was,

he said, more than to stay
in the body
all the way

to the grave, as it happens,
which is what scares us
then and now.

So much for the human.
No one more than any
ever did anything.

But we'll still talk about it,
as if to get out of it,
be God's little symbols...

At least to *stand forth*—
walk up the path,
kick the goddamn rock.

Then take deep breath
and cry—
Thank god I'm alive!

IF I HAD MY WAY

If I had my way, dear,
all these fears, these insistent
blurs of discontent would fade,

and there be
old-time meadows
with brown and white cows,

and those boulders,
still in mind, marked
the solid world. I'd

show you these ridiculous,
simple happinesses, the wonders
I've kept hold on

to steady the world—
the brook, the woods,
the paths, the clouds, the house

I lived in,
with the big barn
with my father's sign on it:

FOUR WINDS FARM.
What life ever is
stays in them.

You're young, like
they say. Your life
still comes to find

me—my honor
its choice. Here is the place
we live in

day by day, to learn
love, having it,
to begin again

again. Looking up,
this sweet room
with its colors, its forms,

has become you—
as my own life
finds its way

to you also,
wants to haul
all forward

but learns to let go,
lets the presence
of you be.

If I had my way, dear,
forever there'd be
a garden of roses—

on the old player piano
was in the sitting room
you've never seen nor will now see,

nor my mother or father,
or all that came after,
was a life lived,

all the labor, the pain?
the deaths, the wars,
the births

of my children? On
and on then—
for you and for me.

ONE

There are no words I know
tell where to go and how,
or how to get back again
from wherever one's been.

They don't keep directions
as tacit information.
Years of doing this and that
stay in them, yet apart.

As if words were things,
like anything. Like this one—
s i n g l e—
sees itself so.

THE FACT

Think of a grand metaphor
for life's décor,
a party atmosphere
for all you love or fear—

let a daydream
make factual being,
nightmare be where
you live then.

When I'm sufficiently depressed,
I change the record,
crawl out into air,
still thankful it's there.

Elsewise the nuttiness of existence
truly confuses—
nowhere to eat
if thousands starving give you meat,

nowhere to sit
if thousands die for it,
nowhere to sleep
if thousands cannot.

Thousands, millions, billions
of people die, die,
happy or sad, starved, murdered,
or indifferent.

What's the burden then
to assume,
as 'twere load on back—
a simple fact?

Will it be right
later tonight,
when body's dumped its load
and grown silent,

when hairs grow on
in the blackness
on dead or living face,
when bones creak,

turning in bed, still alive?
What is the pattern,
the plan, makes it right
to be alive,

more than *you are*,
if dying's the onus
common to all of us?
No one gets more or less.

Can you hurry through it,
can you push and pull
all with you,
can you leave anything alone?

Do you dare to
live in the world,
this world,
equal with all—

or, thinking, remembering,
$1 + 1 = 2,$
that sign means one and one,
and two, are the same—

equality!
"God shed his grace on thee…"
How abstract
is that fucking fact.

PRAYER TO HERMES
for Rafael Lopez-Pedraza

Hermes, god
of crossed sticks,
crossed existence,
protect these feet

I offer. Imagination
is the wonder
of the real, and I am
sore afflicted with

the devil's doubles,
the twos, of this
half-life,
this twilight.

Neither one nor two
but a mixture
walks here
in me—

feels forward,
finds behind
the track, yet
cannot stand

still or be here
elemental, be more
or less a man,
a woman.

What I understand
of this life,
what was right
in it, what was wrong,

I have forgotten
in these days
of physical change.
I see the ways

of knowing, of
securing, life grow
ridiculous. A weakness,
a tormenting, relieving weakness

comes to me. My hand
I see at arm's end—
five fingers, fist—
is not mine?

Then must I forever
walk on, *walk on*—
as I have and
as I can?

Neither truth, nor love,
nor body itself—
nor anyone of any—
become me?

Yet questions
are tricks,
for me—
and always will be.

This moment the grey,
suffusing fog
floats in the quiet courtyard
beyond the window—

this morning grows now
to noon, and somewhere above
the sun warms the air
and wetness drips as ever

under the grey, diffusing
clouds. This weather,
this winter, comes closer.
This—*physical* sentence.

I give all
to you, hold
nothing back,
have no strength to.

My luck
is your gift,
my melodious
breath, my stumbling,

my twisted commitment,
my vagrant
drunkenness, my confused
flesh and blood.

All who know me
say, *why* this man's
persistent pain, the scarifying
openness he makes do with?

Agh! brother spirit,
what do they know
of whatever *is* the instant
cannot wait a minute—

will find heaven in hell,
will be there again even now,
and *will* tell of itself
all, *all* the world.

MiRRORS

In Mirrours, there is the like
Angle of Incidence, from the Object
to the Glasse, and from the Glasse
to the Eye.

—Francis Bacon

One

FIRST RAIN

These retroactive small
instances of feeling

reach out for a common
ground in the wet

first rain of a faded
winter. Along the grey

iced sidewalk revealed
piles of dogshit, papers,

bits of old clothing, are
the human pledges,

call them, "We are here and
have been all the time." I

walk quickly. The wind
drives the rain, drenching

my coat, pants, blurs
my glasses, as I pass.

MEMORY, 1930

There are continuities in memory, but
useless, dissimilar. My sister's

recollection of what happened won't
serve me. I sit, intent, fat,

the youngest of the suddenly
disjunct family, whose father is

being then driven in an ambulance
across the lawn, in the snow, to die.

THE EDGE

Long over whatever edge,
backward a false distance,
here and now, sentiment—

to begin again, forfeit
in whatever sense an end,
to give up thought of it—

hanging on to the weather's edge,
hope, a sufficiency, thinking
of love's accident, this

long way come with no purpose,
face again, changing,
these hands, feet, beyond me,

coming home, an intersection,
crossing of one and many,
having all, having nothing—

Feeling thought, heart, head
generalities, all abstract—
no place for me or mine—

I take the world and lose it,
miss it, misplace it,
put it back or try to, can't

find it, fool it, even feel it.
The snow from a high sky,
grey, floats down to me softly.

This must be the edge
of being before the thought of it
blurs it, can only try to recall it.

SONG

Love has no other friends
than those given it, as us,
in confusion of trust and dependence.

We want the world a wonder
and wait for it to become one
out of our simple bodies and minds.

No doubt one day it will
still all come true as people
do flock to it still until

I wonder where they'll all find room
to honor love in their own turn
before they must move on.

It's said the night comes
and ends all delusions and dreams,
in despite of our present sleeping.

But here I lie with you
and want for nothing more
than time in which to—

till love itself dies with me,
at last the end I thought to see
of everything that can be.

No! All vanity, all mind flies
but love remains, love, nor dies
even without me. Never dies.

THE VIEW

Roof pours upward,
crisscrossed with new
snow on cedar shingles
—grey-black and white—
blue over it, the
angle of looking through
window past the grape ivy
hanging from the top of it,
orange shaded light on,
place fixed by seeing
both to and from,
ignoring bricked window arch
across, just covered by
the light vertically striped
pinned to cross-rod curtain.

HUMAN SONG

What would a baby be
if we could see
him be, what would he be.

What stuff made of,
what to say to us,
that first moment.

From what has come.
Where come from—
new born babe.

What would he like,
would like us.
Would us like him.

Is he of pleasure, of pain,
of dumb indifference
or mistake made, made.

Is he alive or dead,
or unbegun, in between time
and us. Is he one of us.

Will he know us
when he's come,
will he love us.

Will we love him.
Oh tell us, tell us.
Will we love him.

TIME

for Willy

Out window roof's slope
of overlapped cedar shingles
drips at its edges, morning's still

overcast, grey, Sunday—
goddamn the god that will not
come to his people in their want,

serves as excuse for death—
these days, far away, blurred world
I had never believed enough.

For this wry, small, vulnerable
particular child, my son—
my dearest and only William—

I want a human world, a
chance. Is it my age
that fears, falters in some faith?

These ripples of sound, poor
useless prides of mind,
name the things, the feelings?

When I was young,
the freshness of a single
moment came to me

with all hope, all tangent wonder.
Now I am one, inexorably
in this body, in this time.

All generality? There is
no one here but words,
no thing but echoes.

Then by what imagined right
would one force another's life
to serve as one's own instance,

his significance be mine—
wanting to sing, come
only to this whining sickness...

*Up from oneself physical
actual limit to lift
thinking to its intent*

*if such in world there is
now all truth to tell
this child is all it is*

or ever was. The place of
time oneself in the net
hanging by hands will

finally lose their hold,
fall. Die. Let this son
live, let him live.

SELF-PORTRAIT

He wants to be
a brutal old man,
an aggressive old man,
as dull, as brutal
as the emptiness around him,

He doesn't want compromise,
nor to be ever nice
to anyone. Just mean,
and final in his brutal,
his total, rejection of it all.

He tried the sweet,
the gentle, the "oh,
let's hold hands together"
and it was awful,
dull, brutally inconsequential.

Now he'll stand on
his own dwindling legs.
His arms, his skin,
shrink daily. And
he loves, but hates equally.

GREETING CARD
for Pen

Expect the unexpected
and have a happy day...

Know love's surety
either in you or me.

Believe you are always
all that human is

in loyalty, in generosity,
in wise, good-natured clarity.

No one more than you
would be love's truth—

nor less
deserve ever unhappiness.

Therefore wonder's delight
will make the way.

Expect the unexpected
and have a happy day...

PROSPECT

Green's the predominant color here,
but in tones so various, and muted

by the flatness of sky and water,
the oak trunks, the undershade back of the lawns,

it seems a subtle echo of itself.
It is the color of life itself,

it used to be. Not blood red,
or sun yellow—but this green,

echoing hills, echoing meadows,
childhood summer's blowsiness, a youngness

one remembers hopefully forever.
It is thoughtful, provokes here

quiet reflections, settles the self
down to waiting now apart

from time, which is done,
this green space, faintly painful.

THE SOUND

Early mornings, in the light still
faint making stones, herons, marsh
grass all but indistinguishable in the muck,

one looks to the far side, of the sound, the sand
side with low growing brush and
reeds, to the long horizontal of land's edge,

where the sea is, on that
other side, that outside, place of
imagined real openness, restless, eternal ocean.

RETROSPECT

Thanks for
what will be
the memory
if it is.

ONE WORLD

Tonight possibly they'll
invite us down to the barricades
finally sans some tacit
racism or question of our authenticity.

No one will be ashamed he
has to face the prospect
of being blown up alone in
the privacy of his own home.

One can be looted, burned,
bombed, etc., in company,
a Second World War sequel for real,
altogether, now and forever.

MONEY

Stand up, heart, and take it.
Boat tugs at mooring.
Just a little later, a little later.

More you wanted, more you got.
The shock of recognition, like they say,
better than digitalis.

You want that sailboat sailing by?
Reach out and take it
if you can, if you must.

You talk a lot to yourself
about what you don't want
these days, adding up figures, costs.

Here in the rented house on the water
for the proverbial two months,
it's still not enough.

YOU

You will remember little of yourself
as you used to be. One expects this

familiar human convenience. I want
a more abrupt person, more explicit.

Nothing you did was lost, it was
real as you were, and are. But

this present collection of *myselves*
I cannot distinguish as other than

a collection. You talk to yourself
and you get the answers expected.

But oneself is real. There is, presumably,
all that is here to prove it.

MOTHER'S VOICE

In these few years
since her death I hear
mother's voice say
under my own, I won't

want any more of that.
My cheekbones resonate
with her emphasis. Nothing
of not wanting only

but the distance there from
common fact of others
frightens me. I look out
at all this demanding world

and try to put it quietly back,
from me, say, thank you,
I've already had some
though I haven't

and would like to
but I've said no, she has,
it's not my own voice anymore.
It's higher as hers was

and accommodates too simply
its frustrations when
I at least think I want more
and must have it.

DREAMS

I was supposed to wake
but didn't, slept
seeing the separate
heads and faces,

the arms, the legs,
the parts of a person
specific. As always
one was taken

to the end, the place
where the horror dawns
and one has killed
or been killed.

Then to wake up would be
no help in time.
The grey light breaks into
dawn. The day begins.

OUTSIDE

The light now meets
with the shuddering branch.
What I see
distorts the image.

This is an age
of slow determinations,
goes up the stairs
with dulled will.

Who would accept death
as an end
thinks he can
do what he wants to.

THERE

With all I know
remembering a page
clear to my eye
and in my mind

a single thing
of such size
it can find
no other place—

Written word
once so clear
blurred content
now loses detail.

THE VISIT

No resolution,
understanding
when she comes
abrupt, final

anger, rage
at the painful
displacement,
the brutal use

of rational love,
the meagerness
of the intentional
offering.

VERSIONS

after Hardy

Why would she come to him,
come to him,
in such disguise

to look again at him—
look again—
with vacant eyes—

and why the pain still,
the pain—
still useless to them—

as if to begin again—
again begin—
what had never been?

.

Why be
persistently
hurtful—
no truth
to tell
or wish to?
Why?

.

The weather's still grey
and the clouds gather
where they once walked
out together,

greeted the world with
a faint happiness,
watched it die
in the same place.

DEATH

Once started nothing stops
but for moment
breath's caught time
stays patient.

THERE IS WATER

There is water
at road's end
like a shimmer,
a golden opening,

if sun's right
over trees
where the land
runs down

some hill
seeming to fall
to a farther reach
of earth but

no woods left
in the surrounding
wet air. Only the heavy
booming surf.

AGE

He is thinking of everyone
he ever knew
in no order, lets
them come or go

as they will. He wonders
if he'll see them again,
if they'll remember him,
what they'll do.

There's no surprise now,
not the unexpected
as it had been. He's agreed
to being more settled.

Yet, like they say, as he
gets older, he knows
he won't expect it, not
the aches and pains.

He thinks he'll hate it
and when he does die
at last, he supposes
he still won't know it.

BOX

Say it,
you're afraid

but of what
you can't locate.

You love yet
distracted fear

the body's change,
yourself inside it.

Two

OH LOVE

My love is a boat
floating
on the weather, the water.

She is a stone
at the bottom of the ocean.
She is the wind in the trees.

I hold her
in my hand
and cannot lift her,

can do nothing
without her. Oh love,
like nothing else on earth!

WIND LIFTS

Wind lifts lightly
the leaves, a flower,
a black bird

hops up to the bowl
to drink. The sun
brightens the leaves, back

of them darker branches,
tree's trunk. Night is still
far from us.

THE MOVIE RUN
BACKWARD

The words will one day come
back to you, birds returning,
the movie run backward.

Nothing so strange in its talk,
just words. The people
who wrote them are the dead ones.

This here paper talks like anything
but is only one thing,
"birds returning."

You can "run the movie
backward" but "the movie run
backward." The movie run backward.

BRESSON'S MOVIES

A movie of Robert
Bresson's showed a yacht,
at evening on the Seine,
all its lights on, watched

by two young, seemingly
poor people, on a bridge adjacent,
the classic boy and girl
of the story, any one

one cares to tell. So
years pass, of course, but
I identified with the young,
embittered Frenchman,

knew his almost complacent
anguish and the distance
he felt from his girl.
Yet another film

of Bresson's has the
aging Lancelot with his
awkward armor standing
in a woods, of small trees,

dazed, bleeding, both he
and his horse are,
trying to get back to
the castle, itself of

no great size. It
moved me, that
life was after all
like that. You are

in love. You stand
in the woods, with
a horse, bleeding.
The story is true.

AMBITION

Couldn't guess it,
couldn't be it—

wasn't ever
there then. Won't

come back, don't
want it.

FORT COLLINS REMEMBERED

To be backed
down the road
by long view

of life's imponderable
echo of time spent
car's blown motor

town on edge of
wherever fifty
bucks you're lucky.

BEYOND

Whether in the world below or above,
one was to come to it,
rejected, accepted, in some

specific balance. There was to be
a reckoning, a judgment
unavoidable, and one would know

at last the fact of a life lived,
objectively, divinely, as it were,
acknowledged in whatever faith.

So that looking now for where
"an ampler aether clothes the meads with roseate light,"
or simply the "pallid plains of asphodel,"

the vagueness, the question, goes in,
discovers only emptiness—as if
the place itself had been erased,

was only forever an idea and
could never be found nor had it been.
And there was nothing ever beyond.

STONE

Be as careful, as rational,
as you will but know
nothing of such kind is true

more than fits the skin
and so covers what's within
with another soft covering

that can leave the bones alone,
that can be as it will alone,
and stays as quiet, as stable, as stone.

ELEMENTS

Sky cries down
and water looks up.

Air feels everywhere
sudden bumps, vague emptiness.

Fire burns. Earth is left
a waste, inhuman.

STILL TOO YOUNG

I was talking to older
man on the phone

who's saying something
and something are five

when I think it's four,
and all I'd hoped for

is going up in abstract smoke,
and this call is from California

and selling a house,
in fact, two houses,

is losing me money more
than I can afford to,

and I thought I was winning
but I'm losing again

but I'm too old to do it again
and still too young to die.

SAD ADVICE

If it isn't fun, don't do it.
You'll have to do enough that isn't.

Such is life, like they say,
no one gets away without paying

and since you don't get to keep it
anyhow, who needs it.

TWO KIDS

Two kids, small
black sculpture. In
trepidation she turns

to him who bends
forward to, as they say,
assist her. It is,

the proposal is,
her fear provokes her,
fear of a frog

crouching at the far
end of this banal, small,
heavy hunk of metal

must have cost a
pretty penny so
to arouse in mind's

back recesses
a comfortable sense
of incest? Or else

the glass table top on which it sits
so isolates this meager action
—or else the vegetation,

the fern stalks, beside them
hang over, making privacy
a seeming thought

of these two who,
as Keats said, will never move
nor will any of it

213

beyond the moment,
the small minutes of some hour,
like waiting in a dentist's office.

WISHES
for John and Debora Daley

Lunch with its divers
orders of sliced
chicken going by on

the lazy susan with
the cucumber, the goat cheese,
the remnants of the rice

salad left from last night.
All in a whirl the participants
and their very young

children eat, and
drink, and watch for
the familial move will

betoken home ground
in the heat of sultry summer
through the wall-to-wall

glass and beyond to the oaks,
the exhilarated grass, the
fall-off to the marshy

waters, the long-legged white
birds spearing fish
Are we not well met

here, factually nowhere
ever known to us before,
and will we not forever

now remember this? One wonders,
and hopes, loves, conjectures
as to the lives of others,

all others, from other worlds
still here and always
everywhere about us, none

to be left out. No
memory, no thought,
less. Nothing forgot.

ECHOES

Step through the mirror,
faint with the old desire.

Want it again,
never mind who's the friend.

Say yes to the wasted
empty places. The guesses

were as good as any.
No mistakes.

SUMMER

The last waltz
pale days
jesus freaks
empty hours

of sitting around
thinking and drinking
being home
in a rented house

for the summer only
while the folks are away
and we get to use it
so long as we pay.

IF

If your hair was brown
and isn't now,
if your hands were strong
and now you falter,

if your eyes were sharp
and now they blur,
your step confident
and now it's careful—

you've had the world,
such as you got.
There's nothing more,
there never was.

IF HAPPINESS

If happiness were
simple joy, bird,

beast or flower
were the so-called world

here everywhere
about us,

then love were as true
as air, as water—

as sky's light, ground's
solidness, rock's hardness,

for us, in us,
of us.

WAITING

Were you counting the days
from now till then

to what end,
what to discover,

which wasn't known
over and over?

STILL DANCERS

Set the theme
with a cadence
of love's old
sweet song—

No harm in
the emotional
nor in remembering all
you can or want to.

Let the faint, faded music
pour forth its wonder
and bewitch whom it will,
still dancers under the moon.

THE FACES

The faces with anticipated youth
look out from the current
identifications, judge or salesman,
the neighbor, the man who killed,

mattering only as the sliding world
they betoken, the time it never
mattered to accumulate, the fact that
nothing mattered but for what one

could make of it, some passing,
oblique pleasure, a pain immense
in its intensity, a sly but
insistent yearning to outwit it

all, be different, move far, far
away, avoid forever the girl
next door, whose cracked, wrinkled
smile will still persist, still know you.

TO SAY IT

Just now at five
the light's caught the north
side of the trees next
door, the extensive

lawn to the sea's
edge where the marsh grass
seems a yellowish
green haze in late

afternoon. Above, the clouds
move over, storm's edge
passes in bunches of fluffy
soft dark-centered blobs,

all going or gone
as the wind freshens
from the land, blowing out
to sea. Now by the edge

of the window glass at the level
of the floor the grass
has become particularized
in the late light, each

edge of grass stalk
a tenacious fact of being there,
not words only, but only words,
only these words, to say it.

If, as in a bottle, the message
has been placed, if air, water
and earth try to say so with
human agency, no matter the imperfect,

useless gesture, all that is lost,
or mistaken, the arrogance
of trying to, the light comes again,
comes here, after brief darkness is still here.

SOME ECHO

The ground seems almost stolid
alongside the restless water,
surface now rippled by wind
echoed by the myriad tree branches—

and thought is a patient security then,
a thing in mind at best or else
some echo of physical world
it is but can know nothing of.

Three

SUCH FLOWERS

Such flowers can bloom
blurred harsh

winter days
in house so

quietly empty.
Delight in leaves

uplifting to
cold neon or gangling

out toward faint
grey window light.

BUFFALO EVENING

Steady, the evening fades
up the street into sunset
over the lake. Winter sits

quiet here, snow piled
by the road, the walks stamped
down or shoveled. The kids

in the time before dinner are
playing, sliding on the old ice.
The dogs are out, walking,

and it's soon inside again,
with the light gone. Time
to eat, to think of it all.

WINTER

Snow lifts it
by slowing

the movement expected,
makes walking

slower, harder,
makes face ache,

eyes blur, hands fumble,
makes the day explicit,

the night quiet,
the outside more so

and the inside glow
with warmth, with people

if you're lucky, if
world's good to you,

won't so simply
kill you, freeze you.

ALL THE WAY

Dance a little,
don't worry.

There's all the way
till tomorrow

from today
and yesterday.

Simple directions, direction,
to follow.

KID

Smaller, no recall
of not liking one's mother

given as god was
there and forever

loving learned from her
care, bemused

distraction and
much else.

EARLY READING

Break heart, peace,
shy ways of holding
to the meager thing.

Little place in mind
for large, expansive counters
such as Hulme would also

seemingly deny yet afford
with bleak moon late
rising on cold night's field.

BESIDE HER TO LIE

He'd like the edge
of her warmth here
"beside her to lie"

in trusting comfort
no longer contests
he loves and wants her.

CIRCLES

I took the test
and I'm not depressed.

I'm inside here,
I've locked the door,

become a tentative
security system,

sensory alerts, resonant
echoes, lights, long

empty hallways. Waves
crash against the breakwater.

It's dark out there
they think until daylight

lets them off the hook
again till the phone rings,

someone passing
looks in.

ON PHRASE FROM
GINSBERG'S *KADDISH*

"All girls grown old…"
broken, worn out

men, dead
houses gone, boats sunk

jobs lost, retired
to old-folks' home.

Eat, drink,
be merry, you fink.

WORRY

So careful
of anything

thought of,
so slow

to move
without it.

COMING HOME

Saturday late afternoon
with evening soon coming

grey the feel of it
snow underfoot still

weather's company
despite winter's harshness

coming up the path
with the dogs barking

home is where the heart is
this small house stays put.

BE OF GOOD CHEER

Go down obscurely,
seem to falter

as if walking into water
slowly. Be of good cheer

and go as if indifferent,
even if not.

There are those before you
they have told you.

HELP HEAVEN

Help heaven up out
of nothing before it
so deep and soft
lovely it feels to
be here at all now.

SHE IS

Far from me
thinking
her long
warmth, close-

ness, how
her face lights,
changes, how
I *miss* her,

want no
more time
without
her.

OH

Oh like a bird
falls down

out of air,
oh like a disparate

small snowflake
melts momently.

PROVINCETOWN

Could walk on water backwards
to the very place
and all around was sand
where grandma dug, bloomers up,
with her pail, for clams.

N. TRURO LIGHT—1946

Pushing it back to
night we went

swimming in the dark
at that light

house in N. Truro
with that Bill singing,

whistling on, later stuck
his head out subway train

N.Y. window, got killed on post,
smashed, he whistled

out there in the water
Beethoven's Ninth, we

couldn't see him, only
hear him singing on.

RACHEL HAD SAID
for R. G.

Rachel had said
the persons of her life
now eighty and more
had let go themselves

into the *larger* life,
let go of it, *them*
were persons personal,
let flow so, flower,

larger, more in it,
the garden, desire,
heaven's imagination
seen in being

here among us every-
where in open
wonder about them, in
pain, in pleasure, blessed.

QUESTION

Water all around me
the front of sky ahead
sand off to the edges
light dazzle wind

way of where waves of
pleasure it can be here
am I dead or alive
in which is it.

TELL STORY

Tell story
simply
as you know
how to.

This road
has ending,
hand
in hand.

Coda

OH MAX

1.

Dumbass clunk plane "American
Airlines" (well-named) waits at gate

for hour while friend in Nevada's
burned to ash. The rabbi

won't be back till Sunday.
Business lumbers on

in cheapshit world of
fake commerce, *buy and sell,*

what today, what
tomorrow. Friend's dead—

out of it, won't be back
to pay phoney dues. The best

conman in country's
gone and you're left in

plane's metal tube squeezed out
of people's pockets, pennies

it's made of, *big bucks,*
nickels, dimes all the same.

You won't understand it's forever—
one time, just *one time*

you get to play,
go for broke, *forever,* like

old-time musicians,
Thelonious, Bud Powell, Bird's

horn with the chewed-through reed,
Jamaica Plain in the '40s

—Izzy Ort's, The Savoy. Hi Hat's
now gas station. It goes fast.

Scramble it, make an omelet
out of it, for the hell of it. Eat

these sad pieces. Say it's
paper you wrote the world on

and guy's got gun to your head—
go on, he says, *eat it...*

You can't take it back.
It's gone. Max's dead.

2.

What's memory's
agency—why so much
matter. Better remember

all one can forever—
never, *never* forget.
We met in Boston,

1947, he was out of jail
and just married, lived
in sort of hotel-like

room off Washington Street,
all the lights on,
a lot of them. I never

got to know her well,
Ina, but his daughter
Rachel I can think of

now, when she was 8,
stayed with us, Placitas, wanted bicycle,
big open-faced kid, loved

Max, her father, who,
in his own fragile way,
was good to her.

In and out
of time, first Boston,
New York later—then

he showed up in N.M.,
as I was leaving, 1956,
had the rent still paid

for three weeks on
"The Rose-Covered Cottage" in Ranchos
(where sheep ambled o'er bridge)

so we stayed,
worked the street, like they say,
lived on nothing.

Fast flashes—the women
who love him, Rena, Joyce,
Max, the *mensch,* makes

poverty almost fun,
hangs on edge, keeps traveling.
Israel—they catch him,

he told me, lifting
a bottle of scotch at the airport,
tch, tch, let him stay

(I now think) 'cause
he wants to.
Lives on kibbutz.

So back to New Mexico,
goyims' Israel sans the plan
save Max's ("Kansas City," "Terre Haute")

New Buffalo (friend told me
he yesterday saw that on bus placard
and thought, that's it! Max's place).

People and people and people.
Buddy, Wuzza, Si
Perkoff, and Sascha,

Big John C., and Elaine,
the kids. Joel and Gil,
LeRoi, Cubby, back and back

to the curious end
where it bends away into
nowhere or Christmas he's

in the army, has come home,
and father, in old South Station,
turns him in as deserter, ashamed,

ashamed of his son. Or the man
Max then kid with his papers
met nightly at Summer Street

subway entrance and on Xmas
he gives him a dime for a tip…
No, old man, your son

was not wrong. "America"
just a vagueness, another place,
works for nothing, gets along .

3 .

In air
there's nowhere
enough not
here, nothing

left to speak
to but you'll
know as plane
begins its

descent, like
they say, it
was the place
where you were,

Santa Fe
(holy fire) with
mountains
of blood.

4.

Can't leave, never could,
without more, just
one more

for the road.
Time to go makes
me stay—

Max, *be happy,*
be good, broken
brother, *my man,* useless

words
now
forever.

> —*for Max Finstein died circa 11:00 a.m.*
> *driving truck (Harvey Mudd's) to*
> *California—near Las Vegas—3/17/82.*

INDEX
of titles (in capitals) and first lines

241

243

ACKNOWLEDGMENTS

Grateful acknowledgment is made to the editors and publishers of the following publications, in which some of the poems in this book first appeared: *Agenda* (London), *The American Poetry Review, The Atlantic Review* (England), *Attaboy, Atropos* (Montreal), *Bezoar, Black Mountain II Review, Bombay Gin, Boundary 2, The CoEvolution Quarterly/Journal for the Protection of All Beings, Choice, Conjunctions, The Face of Poetry* (La-Verne H. Clark, Ed.; Gallimaufry Press), *Foot, Hard Press, Harvard Magazine, Impact, Ink, International Herald Tribune, Lettera* (Cardiff, Wales), *Little Caesar, Milk Quarterly, Mother's Voice* (Am Here Books), *The New Yorker, The Paris Review, Perceptions, The Poetry Miscellany, Purchase Poetry Review, Rolling Stock, Sailing the Road Clear, The Southwestern Review, St. Mark's Poetry Newsletter,* and *United Artists.*

Several of the poems in this book were originally published in various booklets, broadsides, and chapbooks: *John Chamberlain,* Contemporary Arts Museum, Houston, 1975; the New Zealand section of *Hello,* Alan Loney, the Hawk Press, Christchurch, New Zealand, 1976; *Thanks,* Deerfield Press/The Gallery Press, Deerfield, Mass., and Dublin, Ireland, 1977; *Later (1–10),* Toothpaste Press, West Branch, Iowa, 1978; *Just Buffalo,* Buffalo, N.Y., 1978; *Desultory Days,* The Sceptre Press, Knotting, England, 1978; and *Echoes,* Toothpaste Press, West Branch, Iowa, 1982.

The lines from Patrick Kavanagh's "Prelude" on the title page of *Later* are copyright © 1964 by Patrick Kavanagh and reprinted by permission of The Devin-Adair Co., Inc., publishers of the *Collected Poems* of Patrick Kavanagh.